SHAN

PATH

WORKBOOK

PREVIOUSLY PUBLISHED AS 'YOUR SHAMANIC PATH'

PRACTICAL SHAMANIC CEREMONIES AND
SOUL-DOCTORING (PSYCHO-THERAPEUTIC)
EXERCISES FOR LIVING SHAMANICALLY

LEO RUTHERFORD

COVER ART BY HOWARD G. CHARING

Published 2006 by arima publishing

First published, under the title 'Your Shamanic Path',
by Judy Piatus (Publishers) Limited, London 2001

www.arimapublishing.com

ISBN 1-84549-135-1
ISBN 978-1-84549-135-2

Printed and bound in the United Kingdom

Typeset in Berkeley, Odense & Lithos

arima publishing
ASK House, Northgate Avenue
Bury St Edmunds, Suffolk IP32 6BB
t: (+44) 01284 700321

www.arimapublishing.com

Contents

Introduction

Coming from a straight family – lawyers, estate agent – in north-west England, how on earth did I come to be involved in such an unlikely path as shamanism? I was conventionally educated – injurecated as my first teacher Ken Ratcliffe liked to put it – at boarding schools from the age of eight to 18 (a trauma-laden experience) and then I went into engineering. That in itself was a small rebellion of sorts from my family's tradition of profession, but nothing on any early curriculum vitae would have suggested I could possibly end up where I am today, and there is no way I could have anticipated or predicted any such extraordinary change of direction.

Lives are a series of events, errors, accidents, surprises, challenges, successes, failures, catastrophes, struggles and achievements, and mine has run the gamut. Often a difficult situation yields a new and unexpected solution. My struggle to create a decent business out of a run-down, out of date, shambolic little factory led me 12 years later into a midlife crisis of what felt like monumental proportions. Meaninglessness, exhaustion, incompetence in daily life – inability to remember my shopping list in my pocket – isolation, deep grief; these kinds of feelings led me to seek help desperately. At first I got involved in the alternative group-therapy scene in London. This was in 1975/6, the days when some people became therapists after only a weekend's training, and when the shout-it-all-out-regardless form of encounter therapy was popular and supposed to cure all things pro tem.

In 1977, feeling even worse for wear, I landed in San Francisco where I had been invited by a girlfriend I met at Findhorn. Nothing like sex to motivate a change of country and circumstance. I found healing

1

there through the Hoffman Quadrinity Process, a three-month long, highly intensive workout of parental issues, and I danced at Esalen with Gabrielle Roth and for four years participated in many workshops with her, culminating in a six-week training course. Both of these experiences were wonderful and liberating, and helped me begin to get a sense of who – and just how constricted – I had been, and who and how I might become.

Gabrielle was the first person I heard talk of shamanism, and a little later, in the Holistic Psychology MA programme I joined at Antioch University in San Francisco, Joan Halifax came to teach a course. This opened my eyes further and I began to feel there was a whole strand of earthy basic wisdom in shamanism, an area which I had years ago written off as primitive superstitious nonsense. I did a short course with Hyemeyohsts Storm and Harley Swiftdeer, a university course with Prem Das (Paul Adams) who taught the way of the Huichol Indians of Mexico and a two-week wilderness trip with Robert Greenway of Sonoma State University. I also became involved with the local shamanic circuit, and with many people who were also searching for a way which combined earth connection, ceremony and the sacred, psychology and healing of the inner child. I felt I had found a 'home', a place where the things which touched me the most all came together. With the teachings of the medicine wheel, I found a map which helped me put things in place and let go of all sorts of confusions and doubts, complicated theories and theologies. I felt I could now separate wood from trees, babies from bathwater, and find a sense of meaning and purpose in my life, albeit very different from what my early upbringing had programmed me for.

I returned to England in 1983 and set up as a practitioner. Initially moved by my love of theatre and dance, I created a synthesis I called 'Play-World', and organised fun, playful, creative, spontaneity-oriented events which were successful and popular for a time. However, something more called me and I started to offer short workshops on shamanistic themes and found I could take people much further as it gave me a broader set of tools to work with. In 1987 I changed the name I worked under to Eagle's Wing Centre for Contemporary Shamanism, and so it has been ever since.

All teachers teach to learn and, most of the time, teach what we need to learn. I have created 19 year-long Elements of Shamanism courses since 1987 and continue to learn a great deal each time we work through them. Life's great journey goes on and on through chaos, catastrophe, magic moments, love and loss, unexpected successes and surprises, and learning never ends ... The origins of much – though not all – of the teaching on which this work is based is Native American, north, central and south. The particular medicine-wheel teaching set out here is, as far as I know, Central American in origin and was used by the Mayan culture. It was brought to the West in the 1970s by Hyemeyohsts (Wolf) Storm and his apprentices/students Harley Swiftdeer, Joan Halifax, Rainbow Hawk, and others. Storm's autobiography *Lightningbolt* is very informative and interesting and contains much other teaching that is not in this book.

The way I have expressed the teaching and the interpretations are my own. While I have worked with the medicine wheels, they have 'spoken' to me and some of my emphases have changed from the way I was taught. This is how 'good medicine' evolves and changes to suit the needs of the people and the time, and avoids becoming dogma. It is a living teaching and every teacher will add their own unique quality to the melting pot, provided they are in tune with the needs of the moment and not mired in false concepts of orthodoxy.

I hope you find this book both useful and challenging. I hope it will stir you into thinking for yourself rather than accepting consensual ideas. I hope it will – in the personal sense – prove revolutionary, but I will be happy if you just read and enjoy it.

CHAPTER 1

Shamanism

OUR ANCIENT ROOTS are shamanism wherever we live and whatever sort of culture we have grown up in. It is our spiritual heritage. Look back far enough in time and all of us come from shamanistic cultures. Long before such historically recent concepts as organised religion, humans sought understanding and knowledge of the wider universe using a variety of experiential ways and tools which are just as applicable today as ever. These practices are still in use in a surprisingly large number of places in the world and many shamans of indigenous cultures are now teaching Westerners.

The shamanic journey, the trance-dance, the vision quest, the purifying ceremony of the sweatlodge, these are ancient but eternally relevant ways to contact the timeless reality that exists parallel to and just out of sight of the world we so mistakenly call the 'real world'. It is here in the everyday that we experience the reflections of who we are, of our actions, our deepest beliefs, our 'dreams', but it is in the non-manifest world of the spirit that the hidden causal interactions take place. Hidden, that is, until we begin to open the doors and 'see'. That is the ultimate purpose of the path of shamanism.

The struggle to make sense of life in the third-dimensional spacesuit we call a body is as important today as at anytime. One could almost say even more so now that in the 'developed' part of the world we are polluting our home planet and upsetting the balance of nature and our atmosphere as never before. We desperately need a path that can bring us back into contact and communion with the primal elemental forces of life and can show us a way to come back into alignment with the forces that shape and hold our world in balance.

The way of the priestess and priest, as originally intended, was to guide and aid humankind to connection with the Divine, but too often the 'organised' religions have their own agenda which lead to power being taken away from the people and held by those that represent the concept of the religion or belief system. The original inspiration for many religions reflects the ancient timeless ways, but in the West these have long been hidden or changed to serve the conceptual ideology of the patriarchal culture of 'controlling' how humans experience the Divine and live their lives. In contrast, the aim of the shaman is to serve, to help and guide the people to gain their own sense of power, their own connection to Mother Earth and Father Sky, to the Divine realm, and to 'walk in beauty' and 'walk their talk' as increasingly self-empowered, self-actualising, self-mastering people.

The revival in the West of shamanistic ways since the 1960s is reflected in the proliferation of alternative psycho-spiritual books, workshops and courses which has flourished into, in effect, a vast grass-roots university. Although most of these are not shamanism *per se*, they are nevertheless largely shamanistic in their approach in that ·they reflect the ways and understandings of the ancient cultures. This movement towards self-development and spiritual awareness, and potentially a more community oriented way of living, represents a step forward for those cultures which have been the most predatory towards others and towards the earth in the recent past centuries.

Shamanism, 'good medicine', is like tapping into a vast fund of ancient timeless knowledge which can be practised anywhere under any conditions. It is about helping us humans to heal the effects of past traumas, to live in an inner state of balance and harmony while dealing with the challenges and vicissitudes of life, to develop the best in ourselves no matter what comes our way, and it is about the quality of how we relate to each other and to the earth. All this is as important now as it ever has been or will be.

Our ancestors lived in tribes, villages, small groups, close to the Earth and nature. They knew that survival meant knowing the movements of animals, knowing where plants grew and at what times of the year. Humans lived a long time before the great change came when people began to learn to 'control' nature, to create 'agriculture', to husband animals.

The spirituality of our ancestors, the people of the 'old world' has come down to us through all those cultures who still live in an earth-based manner. These shamanic cultures are all over the world – the Americas, Siberia, Lapland, Tibet, Australia, Indonesia, parts of Europe, Africa ... In fact almost anywhere that is not wholly industrialised you will find shamanistic people, and even in the most 'advanced' societies they are there quietly in the background.

We have been left an incredible legacy of spiritual understanding by these people, our ancestors, and it is time for those of us who have been industrialised, de-tribalised, separated from nature, taught the ethics of competition, individuality, guilt, shame, self-denial and self-denigration to look back, remember, in order to move forward into a way of life that is sustainable, because one thing is for certain, our present way of life is not.

The spiritual understanding of our ancestors is fundamentally the same wherever it comes from. Each culture has its accent, but the underlying 'tune' is the same. This is the essence of what it sings:

All-is-One. Everything is energy. Matter is energy in 'solid' form. All is connected in a great web of life. The Creator and the creation are one. The Creator (or Great Mystery/Great Spirit) is in everything and everything is in the Creator. All beings are part of the Creator and are born from 'spirit' to matter and will die and move back into 'spirit'. Life is existence experiencing and exploring Itself.

All things are 'alive' in their own way. Humans are alive for say 70–120 turns of the Earth around the Sun. A moth is alive for one day. A tree can live for a thousand years. A planet can live for millions of years, A sun has a lifetime of billions of years, a galaxy lives for an unknowable time and as for a universe ... Everything is born into material existence and dies back to the formless realm.

The formless realm – ultimate reality – is timeless. Linear time is a function of the third-dimensional mind.

In Genesis is the statement 'In the beginning was God, and the word was with God and the word was God.' Obviously there were no words so what does it mean? The two primal things for existence to exist are energy and consciousness. Energy must have been present because without energy, there is nothing, and consciousness must have existed because without it there would be nothing to know the energy. So let's put it this way: 'In the beginning was energy/consciousness and energy/consciousness was with God and *energy/consciousness was God*. God and energy/consciousness are synonymous. Everything is energy in form, everything is conscious in its own way, everything is an expression of God in manifestation, God and existence are synonymous.

From this point of view, 'God' is very different from the 'big-daddy-in-the-sky', Father Christmas figure beloved of religionists. The real 'God', 'Supreme Being', 'Great Spirit' – or whatever name we might use – is That Within Which We All Live and a Part of Which We All Are. 'We' means us humans, animals, plants, rocks, planets and suns. Many Native Americans call this the Great Mystery, many use other names, but all of them mean 'All-That-Is'.

Shaman

My favourite description of a shaman is someone who walks with one foot in the everyday world and one foot in the spirit world. It sums up so adroitly the union of living with spirit connection but firmly in the ordinary world as an ordinary person. All things, to the shaman, are energy in form. Temporary form as everything changes all the time. It is worth remembering that diesel oil was once living beings that died and became fossilised in rock strata.

Shamanism is the oldest psycho-spiritual practice of the people of planet Earth. It goes back probably 40,000 years and maybe 50,000, although human history is constantly proving to be longer than previously thought, so who knows, it could be more like 200,000 years. The word shaman comes from the Tungus reindeer herders of the Lake Baikal region of Russia. According to the *Encyclopaedia Britannica* it is derived from the verb *sa* meaning to know, as in the French word *savoir* and the Spanish *sabere*. Anthropologists researching indigenous healing practices the world over have applied this term to healers, visionaries, seers and prophets. Hence what we have come to know as shamanism.

The words witch and wizard come from the Indo-European root meaning to see and to know, as found in the French *voir* or the latin *videre* meaning to see, or the German *wissen* meaning to know. In the history of Britain, witchcraft, wicca and wyrd were shamanic paths of knowledge. They were forcibly put aside and made 'evil' by the conquering Christians as part of the imposition of Christianity as a powerful political force over the land. The word wyrd – which was the name of a spiritual path and the practices that go with it – was devalued to such an extent that it remains in our language as 'weird' with no vestige of its original meaning being left.

Traditional shamans' primary purpose was always to keep the people 'in-spirit', connected to spirit, in a state of enthusiasm for life. The root of enthusiasm is en-theos – connected to the divine, inspired (en=in, theos=god). The shaman is the bridge between the visible, manifest, material world which is described by the Mexican word, 'tonal', and the invisible, non-manifest, intangible world called 'nagual'. His or her role – there have been and are many women shamans, the job is totally non-gender specific – is to serve the people by guiding them to include and connect with the subtle, spiritual realm at all times and to take into account the deeper and longer meanings of life, the rivers of evolution, and to see themselves as part of a great unfolding of existence and not to get lost in the small details. You could say by making life 'bigger' they create a sense of long-term morality and caretaking of the Earth and life. This is now so sadly missing in the West as we create such things as global warming and pollution problems which no society with a connected sense of earth, life, and the long term of evolution could possibly let happen. The Native American people have a saying that whatever you do should benefit seven generations to come, and we have to worry about the next one seeing life through without suffering a major ecological crisis.

Parallel realities

Shamans typically divide non-ordinary reality into three other worlds, the upper, lower (or under) and the middle worlds. Each world has its own characteristics and whilst each traveller experiences initially his or her own version, once one becomes a proficient journeyer, it is amazing to see just how connected we all are at these levels. Shamanic journeying really blows the myth of human separateness and shows just how much we really are all connected. In workshops I find that participants learn remarkably easily how to enter another's lower or upper world, travel there and gain helpful information.

The Lowerworld is the place of instinctual knowing where our animal-like powers reside and where we can find practical earthly help and guidance. Travelling to the Lowerworld is like gaining access to our belly-brain. The Lowerworld is the land fairy stories are set in. Seemingly terrible, violent things can happen yet no one is hurt and the 'dead' just rise again when they feel like it. Alice's Wonderland is here and many cartoons are based on this world, and we know how kids love 'violent' cartoons. To young children they are not violent because they do not yet have a concept of pain and death as experienced in a body. Most helping spirits of the Lowerworld take the form of animals, some as humans, and some as mythical beings. Generally speaking, the Lowerworld appears just like a natural landscape in this world, and when journeying everything one experiences is of relevance and has a symbolic or even a literal meaning.

The Upperworld is the home of more philosophical spirit guides, cosmic beings and great wise elders who appear to us usually in human form and whose wisdom is universal rather than specific. Their help and guidance tend to be more general and not as earthly or practical as the Lowerworld. They guide us more towards seeing the overall lessons of an incarnation than what to do about a present problem. In some cultures an expectant mother will journey with the shaman to the land of the unborn to seek the purpose for which the child is being born. The child is then named to reflect the purpose of its birth.

The light in the Upperworld tends to be translucent and pastel coloured, and the feel is often ethereal. In travelling upwards one goes through a membrane which may appear like a cotton-wool cloud in order to get there. One very important point: the Upperworld is not in any way superior to the Lowerworld, the east is not superior to the west. They are complimentary and equal and one would not exist without the other.

The Middleworld is both the everyday physical world that we live in, the world of ordinary reality, the 'tonal', and also a parallel non-ordinary version of our world. It is in this world where psychic phenomena, telepathy, extrasensory perception, thought forms, 'weird' happenings and so on take place, the things we call in current language vibes, hunches, feelings, intuition. It is the world where disease and sickness manifest before moving into the physical body, the world where psychic healers work, and where negative psychic darts are thrown.

In Chapter 5 we will discuss shamanic journeying more fully, with exercises you can do.

Shamanic healing

To the shaman, it is preferable to seek a cure before getting sick. For example, in the old days in China you paid the doctor while you were well. If you became ill the doctor supported you till you got back on your feet.

Shamanic cultures see disease as a result of dis-ease and dis-ease as a result of loss of power (i.e. loss of spirit – loss of spiritedness, or en-theos – enthusiasm), or of an invasive force acting against health. When one feels unwell or dispirited, it is good to go to the shaman and for him (or her) to take a look into your energy field to see if any intrusions may be in there, and to remove them. The Western idea of waiting until the physical body is sick before seeking help is, from a shamanic point of view, totally archaic and crazy.

Consider how you 'see', frame, conceive and structure your world to be. Is your body a machine which needs treatment and pills to make it well or are you an interactive system of energy with power over your own wellness and illness? How much does your state of mind affect your health, for example are you feeling inspired (in-spirit) or dispirited (disconnected from spirit), are you hopeful and enthusiastic or despairing and disappointed? Do you deeply want to live or do you feel like giving up? The shaman sees his first task as to guide you to move into a feeling of connection with spirit-essence as a valued part of All-That-Is, to inveigle you into deeply desiring to become well and live fully, to persuade you that things can change and there is hope and that life really is worth living. In this way s/he engages your whole being in the healing.

In the shamanic way of seeing, illness begins in the spirit – we become dispirited. If not treated it goes into the mind and emotions and we lose our hope for a future and feel down and negative. Only if that is not treated does the illness get into the body and we become physically sick. There is a tradition of shamanic healing which we in the Western world might regard as fakery. However, is it fakery if it works, and if it does not work why would anyone continue to use it over centuries of time? It is good to remember that one of the most prolific healing pills in allopathic medicine is the placebo, and along with it goes the doctor's proverbial 'bedside manner'. The engagement of the mind and spirit, of the patient's belief that things are changed is all important. The greatest effects on our own 'dream' are from our beliefs, emotions and thoughts.

Magical techniques

From the beginning magical techniques have been used to change consciousness, to enter the imagination, to get past the barriers of seemingly separate consciousnesses and to affect the internal processes of another. From shamanic ritual and ceremony to modern-day theatre, ballet, opera, rock concerts, rave nights, illusion has been and is still used to communicate ideas, feelings, thoughts, inner experiences; to teach, to influence, to affect people's reality. Reality is significantly influenced by what you believe it to be. Life is an inner experience and is constantly affected by your beliefs and inner programmes. While you are on automatic stimulus-response, the inner robot will run the show according to its deeply held programmes – your hidden beliefs. In order to 'see' the world of energy interaction you have to break the hold of your automatic self. That is why it is so important to dehypnotise yourself from the consensus and the old family, education and religious beliefs that no longer serve you, and to re-programme yourself for the life you wish to experience. Chapters 3, 4 and 6 address this specifically.

Ceremony and ritual

By using ceremony and ritual we can move beyond the robotic self, creating and entering magical space where ordinary activity is ceased and timeless time is invoked. We enact something which may be meaningless in the outer world but which speaks to our inner being and has meaning for our inner world. 'Normality' is suspended by agreement and we travel in sacred time and space. We suspend the dominance of the ego, the automatic stimulus-response self of busyness, of achieving and trying. It is a time to speak our truth and hear the truths of others, time to pray to the great powers of the universe and to listen to them in meditation, to place our little self in the arms of the Greater Self of Creation.

How we see ourselves is the root of how we experience our world

Here is a story I was told. The Dalai Lama was talking to a group of American psychologists. 'What is the most frequent problem people consult you about?' asked the Dalai Lama. 'Lack of self-esteem,' said the psychologists. 'What's that?' asked the Dalai Lama. The concept was foreign to him. To have self-esteem you have to have a self to esteem that is separate and distinct, and from a Buddhist point of view that simply does not exist. Also as a life issue, self-esteem was not a problem in his culture in the same way as ours because it was multi-generational and there was an accepted place for everyone in the co-operative way of life. Being a basically non-competitive society, there was much less expectation to 'prove yourself'.

In a culture of multi-generational families, one is unlikely to experience loneliness and self-doubt to the same degree as in the nuclear family or single-person household. Not that multi-generational families do not have their problems, but it is important to understand that they are different. Western culture is like a giant experiment in extreme separateness, isolation, division, loneliness, individuality and competitiveness. In multi-generational societies a person experiences more 'we' than 'I', more a sense of tribal or village collective consciousness. The West has gone as far as a society can into isolation with one-parent families, except for having children brought up in institutions while everyone else lives alone.

Lack of self-esteem/self-worth is the crucial centrepiece, the most basic fundamental wounding of us people of the Western cultures. At its root it is a spiritual matter. Often in psychotherapy, self-esteem is looked at as a personality issue, but way before that it is a spiritual issue. How can a person who believes they are a reject of God possibly value themselves? While you hold the beliefs that you were born in sin, are innately evil and descended from ancestors thrown out by God, with your whole sexuality (a very major energy force within you) relegated as bad and shameful, how can you possibly really care for, value and love your self? Perhaps repeating affirmations like 'I am a worthwhile and valued person' can help a bit with reprogramming the surface self, but it seems to me that it is necessary to get into the deep cultural programme handed down from generations of ancestors and learned both subliminally and literally in one's vulnerable formative years. Let us look in more detail at highly influential beliefs that underpin the culture we live in.

Original innate goodness or original sin?

If you grew up a Tibetan, or a Native American, or an Australian Aboriginal before these cultures were decimated, you would probably have been taught of your innate goodness, your oneness with all creation, your special value to the community and to the Divine. Instead, however, you probably grew up in the industrial West where you may have been taught that you were born in original sin and need to redeem yourself to be acceptable in the eyes of God. When you die you are likely to go to hell unless you believe in the Bible and do what you are told. Some difference.

If you are over 50 you were probably taught that, for disobedience, humanity was thrown out of the Garden of Eden by an angry God and that only by obeying the dictates of the church and praying for forgiveness can you atone for your sins. I used to wonder, as a boy, what I had done so wrong. Only if I prayed to Jesus for the whole of my life could I possibly get to Heaven. What of my personal power, self-esteem, inner sense of worth? Indeed what of self-love? Jesus is quoted as saying, 'Love your neighbour as yourself,' but somewhere along the line, the idea of loving oneself got lost. To dare to say that one loved oneself would invite ridicule. Mind you, that's much the same today, isn't it?

So my view of the world was formed under considerable pressure from my 'elders and betters' that I was basically bad. That only by reining in my spirit, my vibrancy, my life-force, my fire energy, and becoming meek, agreeable to what I was told to believe, completely free of such 'evils' as sexual energy, regularly praying to free my soul of its sins, could I become acceptable in the eyes of society, with the prospect of an afterlife in Heaven. Some mind-control.

How we see our world

The Shuar shaman Numi is quoted by John Perkins (see Bibliography) as saying: 'The world is as you dream it.' How we live our everyday life depends on how we 'see', understand, frame, or 'dream' our world internally. In other words, the stories we tell ourselves of how it is, the mythology we hold of ourselves, the vision we have of life, our deep, hidden beliefs, will largely determine the life we experience.

As we see the world, so we 'make it up' for ourselves. When we 'see' a beneficent world of loving, helpful people, places, happenings, 'spirits', so it is likely to arrange itself for us. When we 'see' a world of enemies and fearsome possibilities aggressing against us, so we influence its manifestation and our experience of it. When we 'see' a world run by a terrifying god-figure with damnation at the end of the road if we do not believe what we are told, we tend to manifest a world that supports that view. We make our world with our deepest beliefs.

The dogmatic religious view has held sway for many centuries much of Europe, the Middle East and the lands conquered by Europeans – the Americas, Africa, some of India and Australasia. However, in the last few hundred years the scientific materialist philosophy has lived with it side by side, bringing a more sterilised framework to the 'dream' of the consensual reality.

Myths of our culture – how the culture is dreaming itself

A culture lives by its mythologies, the stories people tell themselves of how it is and how it works. In the words of Carlos Castaneda's don Juan, we are taught to agree with the way the consensus sees reality. From the moment we are born a deep process of hypnosis begins as we are taught – with live or die emotional pressure – how we are to see and feel the world in order to be an accepted member of family and society. This process is politely called upbringing, education, religion, growing up, maturing etc., and we have to learn to agree with the consensus for our very survival. All of life's goodies are given to those who fit in, who become acculturated, 'normal', and those who dare to see and act otherwise and do not conform are deemed mentally unstable and put away 'for their own good', or at best they become society's outsiders and get a very small share of the goodies.

The most pernicious and disempowering myth of our culture is the idea that a person 'should believe in God'. From a shamanic point of view, this is an absurd idea. The very concept that it is possible or relevant to believe/disbelieve in a God has at its root the concept of a separate God. To have to 'believe' – or to 'not believe' which is also a belief – in God, it is necessary to be able to postulate the question, 'Is there a God?' That question itself contains a myth. The myth that God is separate from existence. Otherwise one is asking, 'Do you believe in existence?', and that is a totally unnecessary and irrelevant question. Existence manifestly exists.

For God to be separate from existence, then existence must have existed before God. That means existence is the real God as it existed first and must have created 'God' out of itself. Shamans say God and existence are the same. The Ancient Mysteries all say that the One became – and constantly becomes, and is, The All. Existence is God-in-Manifestation. Quantum physics, too, shows an interactive universe in constant manifestation and change. So what is there to believe or disbelieve in, when we experience existence all the time?

I was watching a fascinating television documentary recently about black holes and the Big Bang. Stephen Hawking's idea is that the universe ends in a gigantic black hole where everything is swallowed up into singularity – a point where everything becomes nothing – and then explodes back into creation. I can imagine atheists having a field day saying that proves there is no God while religionists defend themselves saying, 'Oh no it is God who makes it go bang into creation.' To shamans there is nothing to discuss – the singularity is the Creator as is the Big Bang and the black hole and all the universes in-between.

What has happened is that some religions created a separate God in their own image, a kind of Father-Christmas-for-Adults. The story has gone wrong and has misguided people. The story of Jesus tells figuratively of how formless spirit enters into the limitations of matter to experience itself in the limitation of three dimensions, living in a space suit – the human body. (See Freke and Gandy, *The Jesus Mysteries*.)

The human self is seen as two: the ego-self who walks in the body upon the earth with all the needs and appetites of the body to contend with and with the many trials, tribulations and tests of life on earth; and the higher-self or Logos who stays in spirit and acts as invisible guide – when the earth-self is willing to listen. To become a master of self, the lower-self, slave-self or robot-self, who is governed by appetites and desires, has to die. It is 'crucified on the cross' of the four directions of fire, air, water and earth – so the higher-self, the inner master, can be birthed in its place. That, in very simple terms, is the essence of the myth of the God-man.

Life is a crucifying procedure. Have you noticed? We do not get away with anything in this life, karma – responsive action – gets us every time. Action brings reaction and all circles are completed. We create karma by our actions. Everything we do brings a response from somewhere in the universe and we label it 'good' or 'bad'. It is all karma, the universe's unique and totally efficient feedback system.

We are strung up on the 'life-cross' of fire, earth, air and water, which to us means body, emotions, mind and spirit. We are life's 'victims' until we wake up to the fact that we are here to take our own power as a multi-dimensional master being. We cannot do this and stay addicted to money, power over others, getting-your-rocks-off sex, fashion, impressing others – all the forces of ego-gratification – we have to travel the hard road that takes us to real inner personal power, self-knowledge and self-identity as part of All-That-Is. This costs: it costs us in terms of habits, addictions and indulgence, in terms of being 'nice' and amenable, it can cost us friends and relations, loss of income, lack of job, loss of prestige in the community. It is not some easy road, it is a hard road to take oneself voluntarily out of the mainstream and into the unknown, the road less travelled, the unknowable path. To travel into the unknown is to travel with not much but your instinct and some guidance from others who have travelled before to guide you. But what an adventure.

However, there is an obstacle which seems to me to prevent many from entering the 'road less travelled'.

Rational thinking

Consider yourself for a moment as an explorer who goes exploring life with a map in hand. The map is your past experience and all that you have been taught and told by those who were here before you, it is your 'bible'. It is your guide to the known realms. Now suppose you come to a crossroads – a moment of decision – and you see that the territory of life and the map do not agree, what do you do? Do you adjust your map to the territory and make your decision incorporating the new knowledge you now have? Or do you insist that your map is correct, that it is sacrilege to accept anything different, that your map must be maintained as correct at all costs? If your map shows a way ahead and the territory shows a wall of rock, do you call in the bulldozers and decimate the landscape to make your map correct, or do you explore to find another way? Well it seems to me that in everyday life most of us adjust our map, but when it comes to matters of religion, this rationality goes right out of the window. Now the world must be made to conform to my beliefs and my rational exploring mind must be shut down.

I suggest we Westerners can be like that and that we have a substantial and hidden problem with our rational thinking process. This may sound a really strange statement as, after all, our whole culture tends to pride itself on being based on rationality. But I would like to suggest that we, collectively speaking, are not rational at all. Our science and engineering are rationally based and work well. Our cars motor and our aeroplanes fly, our buildings stay in place and serve our needs well and our financial systems generally hold together – although our stock and commodity markets are highly emotional in nature. (See Chapter 10.)

However, in terms of our spiritual views, (both believer and sceptic) we can still be locked in one way of thinking, and close our minds to the all-embracing view which is what shamanism can offer.

Problems and challenges of today

At this time many humans have become lost in materialism. Our world is deeply troubled and we do not, collectively, know how to begin to address the problems. Politicians cannot agree what the real problems are or even if they are important. Nevertheless our planet is experiencing global warming, our food is increasingly plentiful but decreasingly nutritious, our major illnesses increasingly pernicious. The arms build-up is frightening and suggests a high level of paranoid schizophrenia within the human race. Destruction is happening to the infrastructure of the planet – the rainforests, the ecological balance of nature, holes in the ozone layer, pollution; herbicide and pesticide residues getting into food, reduction of the male sperm count; unhappiness expressed through increasing use by the young of drugs and stimulants, the decreasing quality of water. One thing that is abundantly clear is that many humans are suffering from a crisis of the spirit and there is a deep need of the soul calling out to be addressed.

Let's look at a few potential looming crises you may not have thought of. The aircraft and air-travel industry. The development of air travel in the last 40 to 50 years is phenomenal. Apparently it is now expected to double in the next 25 years or so. Ease of travel to faraway places is wonderful, and I have certainly enjoyed and benefited from it myself, but what about the pollution caused to the upper atmosphere? One day soon this whole industry may have to be regulated and systematically reduced in order to save us from life-threatening problems by destruction above our heads.

The oil industry. Consumption of fossil fuels continues to rise and though some effort is going on to clean up exhaust pollution in industrialised countries and create alternative technologies such as fuel cells, the quantity of vehicles keeps increasing. However, have you been to a third-world country lately? The pollution in places like Mexico City, Manila or Lima, where there are little in the way of controls, is extremely serious – and as 'prosperity' increases it is constantly becoming worse with no end anywhere in sight or even under consideration. 'Underdeveloped' countries are now wanting more of what 'developed' countries have – more vehicles and more electricity generation. Total pollution is increasing, seemingly without end. If the 'advanced' countries actually manage to reduce consumption and pollution, the 'third world' will more than compensate. Meanwhile in 2001, the USA backed out of the Kyoto agreement on reduction of emissions, and has an energy crisis of its own on the West Coast with lack of electricity capacity. It seems that it needs another 14 power stations to be built to satisfy its needs.

The mobile phone and computer industry. There is the frightening possibility of the development of brain tumours from radiation from extensive mobile-phone use. Not just that but we are all receiving increased radiation from the vast proliferation of masts set up to radiate the messages – not a good idea to live near one of these masts. There is also the possibility of radiation problems from long use of computers when sitting close to a cathode ray tube. Like the other nasty possibilities – the BSE crisis, the AIDS epidemic in Africa – there will, of course, be cover-ups. There always seem to be cover-ups by those who would rather we didn't know, and who, presumably hope such problems will somehow go away.

Then there is the finance industry: banks, insurance, and pension schemes. Just suppose that it becomes clear that the airline and automobile industries must be radically reduced for human, animal and plant survival, that mobile phones are so dangerous they must be used only a few minutes a week and that computer use needs to be limited, what happens to the financial world? The whole economic system is geared to everlasting expansion. I speak from years of experience in industry – nothing is more difficult than reducing the size of an industrial enterprise and staying out of bankruptcy at the same time. It means destruction of a large part of several whole industries, a 1929-like situation only worse, without a way out. An unthinkable collapse and reduction in living standards.

One way or another, something like this is a possibility within our lifetimes. This is an enormous challenge. Great change has to take place and we can do it voluntarily or wait till Mother Earth or desperate circumstances of one kind or another force it upon us.

The call to wake up

Waking up means taking oneself on, shining light on the 'mirror of self-reflection', deep introspection to see who you really are and what on earth life is really about. It means looking at the part of oneself that is a stimulus-response machine that responds to life in a programmed manner, repeating dogmas taken on from parents and culture.

The teachings of the shamans come down to us often in the form of mandalas – circular symbols representing the universe – called medicine wheels. These display the powers that work in the cosmos and on earth and the relationships that exist between them. The Kabbala is a way of laying out the same essential teachings in a vertical and horizontal manner. These teachings show how the one source divides and becomes All-That-Is, the multitude of beings, energies, objects that make up the universe. Note that uni means one – the one-verse. Interestingly the word deity often used for God, the Divine, the Creator, actually means two. The primal division of the one into two is when the unity polarises into masculine and feminine. The Trinity of Spirit is seen as The All, the masculine and the feminine, or as expressed in the way of the Tao, The All, the yin and the yang. Except in the masculinised religions where it is seen as The All, the masculine and masculine.

Waking up has to start with each one of us individually. The Western organised mind readily tends to say we need to get the people woken up – if we wake up the politicians they will organise it, pass some new laws and get everyone woken up. It doesn't work like that, it simply becomes more of the same, more dictatorship, more domination from above. A reminder of that is the classic old story of the new dictator who comes to power to wipe away the old corrupt one and bring freedom. Soon he is organising the new freedom with the aid of his army, and, guess what? It's not freedom any more. Waking up can only be done by oneself for oneself. All personal growth and development is just that – personal. All learning is personal, one can learn from a teacher, but the teacher cannot do the work, one has to do that oneself. Imposing teachings on others is imposing – dictating – dominating. In other words, more of the same. Each of us has to learn for ourself, only you can do the work for you.

Most of us sleepwalk through life repeating patterns handed down to us, learnt in our history. How many times have you heard someone spiel off about something and then felt you are listening to someone else speaking through them – often a parent. This is most visible in intimate relationships. There is a saying that at least six people get married at every wedding. The bride and groom and their internalised parents – and to that you can add their whole ancestral line. Unless, of course, they have done The Work and 'erased their personal history'. Then there may be just two of them. Some difference. Don't you feel a marriage of just two would have a better chance than one likely to be full of parental injunctions and ancestral voices?

This book is about doing 'The Work' and that begins with 'erasing personal history', healing the past so the present and future can be free of the ancestral burdens, shame, guilt, unconscious stimulus-response patterns and robotic behaviour. It is about reclaiming yourself from under the mountain of family and cultural conditioning, acculturation, hypnosis, entrancement, even brainwashing, that has constituted much or all of your upbringing, education, religious teaching and training. It is about retrieving parts of your soul, your life-force energy, that you inevitably lost along the way in traumas and moments of life-threatening fear that happen, especially when one is too young to know anything much except the 'now'. When one is very young and helpless and things go seriously wrong, it feels like nothing less than a threat to your very life. This is the kind of moment when soul loss occurs and part of you splits off and you lose a portion of your energy.

Take a reflective look at your life and ask yourself how much of it you actually run and how much of it you walk through partially asleep? How much of your potential energy do you have readily available to you? In times when we touch the magical-child part of ourselves we can get an inkling of just how much more of us there is, how much potential energy we have somewhere hidden away within. In childhood we all touched the magical child readily and frequently – whenever we were fully engrossed in a game, in activity, with no concept in mind of past or future, shame or guilt, should, must or ought, we were simply fully engaged in the joy of the here-and-now moment, without even a glimmer of a sense of 'I', of self-consciousness.

To touch this place as adults tends to be more difficult. Some people do this through risky sports, for example life-threatening mountain climbing or parachute jumping, ocean sailing; some through wild dance; some through writing or reading; some through drugs – a very dodgy route; and some through spiritual practice – a safe and productive route. We all have a tremendous craving for touching the magical, for altered states of consciousness where we are unbounded, for trance states where we touch the spirit world. Putting it simply, we all have a tremendous craving to touch spirit. We may not know it is that, may not be able to verbalise it like that, but that is what it is. We seek our source.

So you want to travel this journey? Does your spirit demand it? Have you had it with ordinary life? Has ego-massage lost its allure? Is it that for you there simply is no other choice? Well this book is for you and it is my hope and my prayer that it serves to stimulate, reflect, guide and perhaps even assist you to move a little along the way.

But don't believe a word of it, please.

Use it, try the exercises, find out by experience, draw your own conclusions, learn for yourself, grow in your own unique way. Life is the journey and your life is yours. Have a good one.

CHAPTER 2

Reality Maps

Teachings of the medicine wheel

I T IS VERY ADVANTAGEOUS when on a journey to have a map. Without a map it is difficult to know which way to turn and the journey can feel like a puzzle, sometimes with what feel like booby traps along the way. With a good map everything becomes much clearer. One still has to travel the journey but a map gives a sense of from where one has come and to where one is endeavouring to go. For me personally, after early years of extreme confusion and puzzlement about Life, the Universe and Everything; about God, religion, sin, and the meaning of life, I was introduced to the medicine wheel and found I had a map. A map is not the territory, but it enables one to look with an eagle's eye. Understanding the map felt tremendously liberating to me and helped me to get a handle on life's puzzle.

There are many ways of teaching the medicine wheel and the one I learned and work with comes from the Americas, probably Central America through the Mayan culture. On this medicine wheel, the south relates to the water element and emotion, the west to the earth element and the physical, the north to the air and the mental realm, and the east to fire and the spiritual realm. The centre is the place where all forces are in balance, the place from which creation flows. The medicine wheel is life in a circle. It is a teaching, a way. It shows our connection to all things, it shows the way back to the centre, our way home.

Medicine means everything that heals. To heal is to be made whole. To be whole, to be fully human, is to be holy. Medicine is strength and wisdom gained through life experience. Medicine is power in the real sense of that word – power over oneself and one's ability to respond to life. Our medicine is what we have to 'giveaway' to the world, to other humans. It is what we contribute to the collective in our lifetime. It is what we look back on at the end of life with pride and pleasure – what we gave to the evolution of All-That-Is, our unique contribution.

The medicine wheel is a circle of knowledge. It is the universe and it is the individual. As above, so below – the greater is reflected in the lesser and the lesser in the greater.

There are four directions – and the centre makes five. Then there is the above and the below – and that makes seven. Seven is the 'dream' of the Creator in manifestation. It is the Creator experiencing him/her/itself. The medicine wheel is a path towards understanding the multitude of powers that create and affect life in the third dimension of material reality.

The east of the wheel is where the sun rises. It is the place of beginnings and endings, of vision and inspiration – where spirit comes into matter and where matter touches spirit – the place that is beyond the confines of linear time. It is springtime and the planting of seeds and the beginning of sprouting. It is the place of eagle and condor who fly between the worlds and see the big picture from high above. It is the place of the Mage or magician, the 'I-mage-a-nation' where we learn that what we imagine can become real. It is the place of the visionary, the one who sees beyond the apparent reality, and of the energy matrix which underlies the physical bodies of all living things. It is the place of the mountain, where we go to be alone and to contemplate Life, the Universe and Everything. It is the fire of spirit where dross gets burned away, but where we need to navigate with care to make sure it is only the dross that is burned. It is the place of men's council and of the *heyeokah*, the contrary-joker-comedian, who teaches truth through showing the world upside down. It is the domain of Spider Woman who weaves her web, continually creating and re-creating the universe, reminding us that the weaver and the web are one.

The south of the wheel is the place of trust and innocence, the time of childhood. It is the place of emotion, energy-motion, of water, of passion and the heart. We learn to touch and be touched, to feel and to be moved by beauty and magic. The south is where the child

26

experiences the world as alive, shimmering and connected, and then is usually taught the adult consensual reality of a dead, disconnected, separate world in which one has to struggle for survival. South is the place where time begins for us and where our past affects the present until we turn the mirror of self-reflection upon ourselves. There is a medicine-wheel teaching which says look at spiritual childhood as lasting until we are about 27, just before Saturn returns to the position it held in the sky at the time of our birth and turns life upside down.

The south is where we experience the warrior's first enemy – fear – and learn to do battle and not be overcome. The animal totems of the south are Little Mouse who reminds us that the big picture is made up of many little details, Coyote who tricks us into all sorts of scrapes from which we learn and grow, and Serpent who sheds his skin and teaches that we too must shed our past to move on and to grow. South is the place of White Buffalo Woman who brings the medicine pipe to the people to teach and remind us of the sacredness of all things.

The west is the place of the setting sun where we draw ourselves inwards to do inner work. This is woman's place, the deep, the dark, the inner, the womb where new creation is nurtured, the place of introspection. The west is the place of Grandmother Earth who gives life and who teaches of cycles and patience, of the permanence of change, of death, decay and rebirth, and that death gives life and all things are born, live, die, decay and give new life. It is the direction of all things physical, of the now, the present moment, which is the only time that physical matter knows.

West is the place of Bear who hibernates for the long winter and dreams; of Owl who knows the night; and of Jaguar who teaches of death and the need to overcome inertia and deadness and become a spiritual warrior, one who knows all 'enemies' are really allies and teachers. This is the place of our spiritual adolescence which can be looked at as the period from about 30 to 54 years of age, the time of apparent maturity in the everyday world during which we are working to achieve real maturity in the inner world.

It is the place of the inner spiritual being of opposite polarity, woman's inner man and man's inner woman, with whom we make contact when we shut out the stimulus of the outer world and touch the silence.

West is the place of changing woman who teaches of constantly flowing and moving cycles, of the continual rhythm of ebb and flow, and of the interconnectedness of all that exists and our responsibility to nurture life and all living things. The west reminds us of our responsibility to our mother, the Earth, who gives us the incredible gift of life, and who constantly meets all our needs.

The north is the place of winter when the ground is frozen and we have to learn to co-operate to survive. It is where we learn to achieve adulthood with maturity and to give way to one another, and that the survival of the tribe, group, village, country and planet is more important than that of any one individual. This is where we learn to plan for the future and to look at how our actions will affect the next seven generations that follow us.

The north is the place of the mind, of thinking, of intellect, of the wind. The animal totems are the Great White Buffalo who gives all of himself to feed and clothe the people and so teaches of the sacredness of the giveaway and reminds us that we, in our turn, give away all we have 'borrowed' from Mother Earth at the end of our time here; Wolf who is teacher, direction finder and keeper of the family; Horse, keeper of wisdom and philosophy, and Dragon who leads us to an encounter with direct knowingness, a face-to-face encounter with power.

North is the place of mystery teachings such as the medicine wheel, the ancient ways of the shaman, teachings of what it means to become fully human – hu means divine, man means mortal. Adulthood can be considered as the period of life from about 57 to 81 years, the time where we may gain the true maturity of spirit in matter. We learn that we are part of a collective and that our individuality is completely interwoven and interdependent with that of our group, our country, all humankind, all kingdoms, the planet herself. This is the time of spiritual maturity as we come to understand that our wisdom, knowledge and experience are to be shared for the good of all – for the survival and thriving of all. The north is the place of Rattling Hail Woman who holds the universe in her hands and teaches that we must be involved in the welfare of all beings.

And so as our life comes towards its completion we come back once more to the east, now as an elder. We can think of this as the period from about 84 to 108 years, or whenever the end comes. This is when we return to the simplicity of childhood as our outer faculties lessen and we move more inward to the essential being who came in at the beginning. All of life leads to death. It is a circle. The teachings say that linear time is an illusion which we experience in the third dimension only. That means that we will step back into the spirit world at the same moment that we left it to come into this world. From spirit's view, our whole life's journey is in the blinking of an eye.

As the end of our life approaches, the fire begins to burn up the matter of our bodies until just the essence is left. The quality of our old age is dependent upon how much we have done to heal and clear our self during our journey, on how much we have kept in-spirit, inspired, in contact with the spirit world, and on how much we have done to develop our gifts and talents and to give them in service to others. In the old cultures, the elders were the Wise Ones who, through the trials and tests of life, gained immeasurably valuable life experience which they made available to the younger generations. This tradition has almost vanished in the 'developed' world – and the 'developed' world may vanish unless it returns.

Each of the directions can be considered as a lodge, a 'home'. The teachings say that we will be 'at home' in one of the four directions, and its trials and tests will be easy for us. Two other directions will require work, but their lessons can be learned with relative ease, but the fourth direction is where our biggest challenges lie and may require our lifetime's work to gain mastery of its lessons.

Each direction has its 'enemy', its challenge, its hook to ego and self-importance. In the east it is spiritual pride, self-glorifying misuse of power, rejection of the earth and matter, and attachment to 'superior spiritual affairs'. In the south it is the self-pitying stories and pain games with which we entertain ourselves and excuse ourselves from responsibility so we can stay in the place of child and avoid actually growing up and tackling the challenges of our lives. In the west it is self-absorption, self-obsession and consequent depression; a refusal to come out of the dark and into the realm of earth experience and to tackle the challenges that life – God – puts our way. In the north it is knowledge without wisdom, intellectual arrogance, dogma, pedantry, theories and concepts adopted without experience; the critical, judgmental mind that destroys the self while it thinks it is cleverly showing its superiority over others.

It is our life task to balance the forces within ourselves and to learn to steer a course through the great maze of manifestation. Each one of us has our own particular journey to travel and each one of us has to make our own decisions at every turn. In childhood there are parents and Father Christmas figures to guide and take responsibility for us. Once into adulthood there is no one there, no big-daddy-in-the-sky, Father Christmas god-like replacement, nothing except our self and our spirit guides, who may guide but certainly do not take responsibility for us. The journey is one of making our own way, through our own choices, our own effort, and taking our own responsibility for the outcome. No one is to blame, there is no blame, there is just experience to be experienced, and awareness, perception and consciousness to be gained. Each direction is a mirror and it reflects to us what we need to know in order to grow and develop and complete our self. Its purpose is to help and guide us to return home to the place of balance, alignment, harmony, and health that is our centre, where our little will merges with the great will of creation.

Medicine wheels have been used for teaching about the cosmos since antiquity. The remnants of stone circles can be found all over the world. The ancients saw their world in terms of circles and cycles, and time as circular rather than linear. Medicine wheels teach of the workings of the cosmos, of the natural order; of the human's place in the natural order and of the purpose of life. They show the powers that hold the universe in balance.

The Medicine Wheels teach us that life is not a philosophical question. Life is our human reality, truth, fact and teacher, no matter how bitter or sweet. The Wheels teach that Life is not a religion. Rather, Life is the perfect opportunity to Learn and Grow by first questioning – asking who each human is.
(Hyemeyohsts Storm, *Lightningbolt*.)

Life works in circles and cycles. All action brings reaction. The usual name for this is karma. It is not retribution, a wholly incorrect teaching, but the natural balancing of the forces of shadow and light, it is the lessons we come to earth to learn and which the universe serves up over and over until we learn them.

Most of us begin as ordinary people under the thrall of everyday culture, governed by our needs for security, approval, recognition and acceptance. We rely on the outside world for a sense of identity and give away enormous amounts of our personal power and sense of right over ourselves.

How sad it is that such a state of affairs should be considered 'normal'. When I am giving a talk I often ask the audience how many of them have ever been in a trance or been hypnotised. Some hands go up. I then ask how many think they have never been in a trance, never been hypnotised or brainwashed. Usually quite a number of hands go up, some very firmly. I then ask, 'But what about the trance you are in right now? The one called normal consciousness?' A laughter of recognition usually follows. I talk about 'normal waking consciousness' as the deepest trance state on planet Earth. For some this is a contentious and challenging idea, but just how conditioned are you? Just how conditioned; hypnotised, entranced are others you know?

Since birth we have been the subject of indoctrination. It is what we know as education, religion and upbringing, and it teaches us how to fit into the family and culture around us. Later in life we may travel to very different cultures and, if we stay long enough, get a sense of how they see the world. Then the chances are good that we will get culture shock on our return home. This is a great opportunity to see just how 'normality' is a cultural phenomenon and not a given absolute and to see just how odd much that our culture accepts as normal really is.

The Red Road and the Blue Road

The four directions form a cross and a cross has two 'roads'. The north–south axis can be called the Red Road, and the west–east axis the Blue Road. In this map, the Red Road is the road of our mental-emotional, adult and inner-child selves. It is the road of thinking and feeling, of looking to the future and to the past, the part addressed by psychology and psychotherapy. The Blue Road is the road of the physical-spiritual, of our spiritual-adult and magical child selves. It is the road of the body and the spirit, the present moment and the timeless, the part addressed by spirituality and by transcendence-focussed physical disciplines such as martial arts.

Note that this is a map, a path to seeing into the matrix. You may find that in another teaching the meaning of the roads is reversed or is perhaps framed differently. All maps are just maps – paths to follow until you no longer need them and can traverse from knowledge and experience. A map is a metaphor, a way of expressing what things are like, of showing connections and opposites, paradoxes and similarities. Please journey through what follows with that understanding.

The red road

The arena of our mental–emotional everyday selves is the Red Road. The north represents our functioning adult persona and the south is the emotional inner child. At any moment it is worth looking at who is boss. Health is a nice balance between the two but when the emotional child gets upset and runs over the adult, we can lose balance and all hell can break loose, whereas when the adult dominates and the child doesn't get a look in, our emotions become stultified and frozen and we lose life energy.

Facing south we see the element of water – the oceans, the rivers, the rain and all that flows. Inside ourselves we are more than 70 per cent water, part of which is our blood which carries nutrients around the body and scavenges what is no longer useful. When we face the south of ourselves, we face our emotions and our past. This is the medicine of Little Mouse who reminds us of the small details. It is the 'close-to' place. Our emotions are formed out of everything that has happened before the moment of 'now'.

The first emotional 'enemy' we all have to work with is fear. Not the physical fear of literal events – that is part of the medicine of the west, but emotional fear. This means shyness, inhibition, fear of not being acceptable, fear of ridicule, fear of emotional insecurity, fear of rejection, fear of being put down, laughed at, made to feel small, belittled, derided, made to feel like a dimwit, clodhopper, greenhorn, ignoramus ... etc. I am going on a bit because this is the fear that is stultifying, dispiriting, emotionally crippling and extraordinarily destructive especially to a vulnerable growing child or adolescent. To an adult it only hurts if one has low self-esteem. A person who truly values him or herself will have no problem with this and realise it is a reflection of the other person's problems. Unfortunately low self-esteem is rather the norm for acculturated Western people.

The 'ally' as taught by the medicine wheel is trust and innocence. This means the ability to trust, to have faith in the universe, to trust in existence, in creation, and one's personal right to exist. This means embracing fundamental self-esteem and self-love as one's right. To live with trust and innocence is to live as a rightful part of creation, of the Creator. To hold at the level of one's deepest being that one is integral with creation, with All-That-Is, and thus is utterly entitled to be, to express, to act in the world, to have a life of one's own, to be free of the internal bondage of other people's beliefs and dogmas, to live one's own choices and take responsibility for one's self.

EXERCISE

Stop for a moment and take your consciousness inside. Feel your being as part of all creation, breathe deeply and feel your weight on the chair or floor. Say to yourself '*I am*', and know you are an equal part of existence and that existence is in you. You are connected to everything, a part of everything; you are not, have never been and cannot be separate from All-

That-Is. Remember that All-That-Is values you as a part of Itself, which is All-That-Is. All-That-Is loves all parts of It's self, and that includes you. You are a loved and wanted part of creation.

The north of the wheel is the place of the element of air – the winds – and for us this is the place of the mind, of thinking and calculating, rationalising and working out. This is the place of 'knowing'. The mind looks to the future to work out what is next and how to create the kind of future we want – unless our self-esteem and sense of worth is screwed up, in which case we are likely to be working subliminally to create a lousy future because our inner hidden dialogue says that this is all we are worth.

The 'enemy' of the north place is usually called the enemy of clarity. There is a lovely piece in one of Castaneda's works, *The Teachings of don Juan*, I think, when don Juan talks about the four enemies of a spiritual warrior. The second he labels clarity, 'the moment when a man thinks he knows and understands is a dangerous moment because that is the moment he closes his mind', is the gist of what he says. When teaching this wheel I have found misunderstandings creeping in as to the advantages as well as the disadvantages of clarity, so I have chosen to rename the enemy 'bullshit' so there is no question or doubt about the meaning whatsoever.

The 'ally' is knowledge, and with it comes the quality of wisdom. Knowledge is that which one truly knows. Not from belief, conjecture, conditioning, training, wishful thinking, brainwashing, nor from anywhere outside oneself, but from inside; tested by repeated experience. Our life is only experience anyway – that is all we have. All our life happens inside, not outside – only the effects happen outside for us to see and respond to. Life itself is an internal experience, and knowledge can only be found inside. Other people's knowledge can be found in books but it is not your knowledge until you actually know it and experience it as living truth for yourself.

EXERCISE

♦ Take a piece of paper and draw a line vertically down the middle. On the left side write down ideas you used to hold as *the truth* but no longer do. For example, God, politics, your worth as a person, what life is really about, what is actually worth doing, what you are living for, what kind of movies are worth watching, etc.

♦ On the right side write down what is *true for you now* in the same areas.

♦ How have you changed?

The blue road

The west of the wheel is the place of the element of Earth and the physical Earth herself. We place our body in this direction as the physical only knows the moment of now, so the time of the west is the present. It is the 'looks within' place, and our personal work is the struggle between life and death. The ultimate death is called by medicine teachers 'death-death', but there are many 'mini-deaths' to be died along the way. Every pattern we change is the death of something old, which makes way for something new. Every dispiriting pattern we fail to change is a nail in our energy body which reduces and deadens our available life force. From an everyday point of view, the tendency towards 'death' with which we struggle is most easily labelled inertia, and the ally we have at our disposal to assist us in this great work is introspection: the willingness to look deep within ourselves, warts and all.

In summary the challenge of the west is our life versus our death, our liveliness and vibrancy versus our deadness and inertia.

How alive and how 'dead' are you? How alive or dead are people you know? How many are full of vibrancy and aliveness and how many are partly dead and inert?

EXERCISE

◆ Take a moment to settle down quietly. Ask yourself, 'How much of myself am I living and how much is remaining dead or unexpressed?' On a scale of one to ten, very quickly let your inner self illuminate a number.

◆ Take a piece of paper and write down what you feel brings you most alive and into feelings of loving life. Then write down what brings you the opposite feelings, into inertia and deadness. Compare.

The east of the wheel is the place of the element of fire, of the non-physical energy of spirit, of timelessness, of imagination and inspiration. It is the 'sees far' place, where we can take an overview of things. The quality of the east is power but the issue of whether that power becomes an ally or enemy is a monumentally important one. Well-used power brings with it a feeling of illumination and a sense of lightness and lovingness with others. Power used to dominate and control leaves no loving space and only heaviness.

The inner aspect of ourselves is the magical child, that part we connect with in play and fun, in dance and celebration. This part has no future and no past, no bonds and no allegiances for gain, it is ourselves when free and fully in-spirit. The magical child can only use power for the good of all, and would not know a manipulation if it fell over one.

EXERCISE

◆ Feel the magical child inside you. An easy way is to remember moments from childhood when you played just for the fun of playing, and there were no agendas, no one to impress, no one to please, just games to be played and fun to be enjoyed. Call such a moment to mind and seek inside yourself for the feelings, the enthusiasm, the love of life. Open your eyes and bring these feelings back with you and hold them inside for as long as possible.

Maps of the journey

There are many ways of going around the wheel for knowledge and illumination – and their opposites – and here are some of them.

♦ We approach life with trust and innocence – inner sense (south) – seeking knowledge (north) wisely in order to see a little further into how things really are (east – illumination), and so we come to feel more alive and vibrant (west).

♦ Conversely, we approach an issue with fear and trepidation, worried about our security (south). We compensate (north) by not allowing our self to see what is true or speak our truth, and then we misuse power to cover up our tracks (east) and end up feeling guilty and deadened (west).

♦ We get stuck in fear of a situation and do not face up to it (south). Secretly we are angry but dare not stand up for our self and show it (north – out of truth). We become stressed with the situation and are at war inside ourself but still cannot resolve it (east – lack of illumination), and end up deadened and depressed (west).

♦ We set about 'erasing personal history' – an aspect of ourself, a bad habit or addiction (south). We dare to look deeply within and face the death of this part of who we have been (west). This enables us to see beyond the cultural mind-conditioning mind-stuff, hence to 'stop the world' (north) which in turn enables us to master a piece of our 'dream of life' and increase our power of choice and self-determination (east).

♦ Seeking to erase a piece of personal history we get afraid and overwhelmed by old parental voices of shoulds, musts and oughts (fear – south). We cannot face the death of this aspect of ourself and resort to old habits and safe patterns (unable to face death – west); thus we cannot stop the world, rather the world reinforces its hold on us (north) and we fail to master our dream of life. Instead it masters us and we lose the feeling of the ability to make our own choices (east).

EXERCISE

◆ Look at an issue in your life right now and see if one of the patterns above reflects how you are handling it. Look for illumination on how you could handle it.

◆ Do this for important past issues. See what you can learn.

WALKING THE RED ROAD

CHAPTER 3

Where does your power go?

Addictions, dependencies, neediness, judgments

WHEN THE COLLECTIVE DREAM no longer works for you, the call has come to change, to awaken, to shine the light of self-awareness upon yourself. Perhaps we are those for whom life has made itself sufficiently untenable, for whom life has pushed to the limits of despair and desperation, for whom life has become unliveable, who turn to seek sense in it. In mythological terms it is those upon whom 'Coyote the Trickster' has fixed his beady eye and his devious doings, or 'Lucifer the Light Bringer' has taken into the darkness and shown a pinprick of light, or whom 'God' has abandoned. One way or another, life has brought us to think again, to question what had been taken for granted, to shine light upon our sacred cows, our cherished beliefs, to truly wonder why we are born and what on Earth we are doing here.

Take a look at yourself for a moment. What brought you to a path of self-healing? Did you reach a point of despair? Did your sense of self-worth, self-love reach such a low ebb that there seemed no point in it all? Did life take you deep into yourself and force you to ask the most difficult questions about your existence, your relationships to other people, to the planet, your reason for being alive? Rarely does anyone step on to a path to seek the light without an experience deep in the shadows. For myself it was periods of deep despair and loneliness that propelled me to find something worthwhile in life if I was to continue.

There is a totally false idea held by 'tabloid consciousness' that working on oneself to heal and help oneself is somehow self-indulgent. This is a quite extraordinary idea and when you consider the opposite, it becomes clear just how insane it is. To not work on yourself, to not self-reflect, to not take responsibility for yourself and learn from your karma – the reactions that come from your actions – means to go out into the world and perform actions which affect others and the earth with no reflection on your real motives, no attempt at self-knowledge. A good example is Hitler who apparently had a most fiendish childhood and then acted out his hatred across Europe. Who knows, if he had had a good therapist instead, the world might have been saved a great deal of pain and destruction. German psychotherapist Alice Miller has written extensively about Hitler.

The Native American phrase *omitaquaye oyasin* means for all my relations. It is traditional to say this when entering a sweatlodge and at other ceremonial moments. It means, 'I do this not just for myself but for all I am related to.' And who are they? They are my blood relatives, all my human brothers and sisters; my animal kin, plant kin and rock kin. It is the whole planet herself. I am related to all that exists. While I am out of balance, depressed, angry or violent, I am a force for imbalance, for anti-life (live spelt backwards becomes evil) and in need of healing. As I heal and balance myself, I become a force for good and healing for others. All self-work is for the good of all. Each self is a cell of the whole.

Infancy

When we are an infant we are truly helpless and dependent upon our mother. She is therefore quite literally to us, 'mother-god'. Later, if we are lucky, we meet another 'god' – our father. To a child, gods can do no wrong. This is very important because it means that when parents fail to be perfect, the child believes it is his own fault. When parents argue or divorce, the child tends to blame itself. This is not logical from an adult point of view, but it is a human fact nevertheless. It is a programme for survival to make us bond at all costs with a nurturer of life; fear of death – non-existence – is quite the most tremendous motivating force.

This existential fear has an enormous psychological component – how could it not? It creates core beliefs – or we could call them core hypnoses. They start very early and subliminally. Little girl is safe with mother and this fierce threatening dark man keeps coming and upsetting the idyll, and mother placates him each time. Message: men are threatening and women must give in to them for security. Little boy with mother, safe and secure; daddy comes home with parcels, presents at Christmas, supplies – and goes out again – he seems to be at home only when he is bringing things. Message: men are providers but they do not really belong at home. Little boy with bossy mother who organises and controls everything in his life. Message: women will take over and control you if they can, better to keep them at arm's length. These are very mild examples of the formulation of hidden core beliefs, but it is these deeply hidden 'myths' that rule until we can stalk them and bring them to the light of day to re-examine them in the present where we have the power of change.

Inside each of us is a formidable being who keeps our life on the road. Well, a road, anyway. The question is how much this is the road on which we really want to travel and how much is it actually someone else's idea of what our road should be. I am referring to our inner automatic, domesticated, stimulus-response machine-self. Our *robot*.

Our robotic self

The robot – sometimes called subconscious mind – runs the show precisely according to the programmes s/he has received over all the years you have lived. The deeper and more hidden the programme, the more energy the robot will exert in seeing it fulfilled. The robot is like an ally of monstrous proportions who is totally dedicated to what it sees as your well-being, who is acting out all your shoulds, musts and oughts – and your shouldn'ts, mustn'ts and oughtn'ts – with vitriolic abandon. There is nothing wrong with the robot, it will always be there. The problem is the programmes. Are the programmes what you want to be living now? Did you put them there yourself? Or are they largely parental programmes, religion's programmes, education's programmes, cultural programmes? Programmes put in by others aided by the enormous stimulus of fear, especially way back when you were truly helpless?

We are all deeply hypnotised beings. Since we plopped out of the womb, the process of indoctrination has been going on. It is to make us entranced by consensual reality so we will become a regular member of society: a regular guy, a regular girl. That is how our parents and elders want it. They want us to grow up and have what they see as a 'good life'; to become a 'credit to them'; to affirm in our way of being their rightness in their way of being. It is perfectly natural but it is nothing more than hypnosis, entrancement and, I will even go as far as to say, brainwashing. The issue at stake for us now is retrieval of our own power over our self, and the making of the robot into our servant and our master no longer. This is the first part of the task of waking up, the task that all spiritual paths teach in their own way. In the shamanic path it is often known by the prosaic title of *erasing personal history*.

Erasing past conditioning

As we grow up we are taught by example, by images, by 'modelling', how we are supposed to become and what is acceptable and unacceptable. It is the parents and close family who form our emotional understanding of the world. One of my teachers, Harley Swiftdeer, calls them the *image makers* on the basis that they make the images which we learn to copy in order to become acceptable adults.

As we grow up it is the family 'image makers' and archetypes who influence our emotional understanding of the world. This is where our conditioning begins. Then in adolescence the peer group becomes all important and the fashion industry and media greatly affect the 'norms' of that period of our life. Fashion is an incredible industry which, if you really think about it, is, at its simplest root, about copying other people. Most of us are desperate to belong, especially if our self-esteem is low, and so these powers are usually enormous in forming how we see and feel the world on the tricky transition from child to adult.

Our physical circumstances are governed by economics and initially by family circumstances. Working in factories I came across many people whose choices were proscribed by the working-class mores of the times. Some possible choices were factory production-line worker, miner, driver, machinist, foundry worker; fodder for some basically mechanical, repetitive and likely soul-destroying activity. The job was something one had to suffer in order to exist and have a place in the scheme of things, and it was assumed very deeply that a person did not have much in the way of rights to upset or challenge that scheme. The recent movie *Billy Elliott* is a delightful story of a miner's son's struggle to break the mould and become a ballet dancer.

The spiritual aspect of life has been controlled by religion, which taught what one should believe. By giving over one's search and leaving it to the church, believing what one was told, one could be 'saved' – saved from the difficult and tricky path of actually looking at oneself and taking responsibility for one's own spiritual development. So self-discovery and self-development were subtly taught as unnecessary, even evil. Just believe and pledge yourself to the church and all will be looked after. No matter how frightful the time you suffer on earth, the promise of life after death sitting on the 'right hand of God' beckons you, provided you obey and do what you are told and don't rock any boats.

The medicine wheel places sexuality in the same corner as spirituality. What a strange combination you might think, but look at it this way. Our sexuality is the most creative part of ourselves. Through sex we create new life, only through sex is our race continued – notwithstanding myths of virgin births. The primal energy of sexuality is also our creative energy, our individuality. It is our sex that leads us on the merry dance of life, that pushes us out to meet and unite with others, that creates the mixing of peoples.

Sex is the great stimulator and mover within each of us. Therefore it is the prime target of those who would seek to control us. There are two paths to world domination. One is the straightforward path of the 'sword' as used by the great empire-building emperors and their conquering armies. The other is with the suppression of sexuality, spontaneity, inner fire, self-determination, creative energy, the right to think and choose for oneself, to follow one's own bliss, the promptings of one's own soul. The weapons for that are shame, guilt and self-blame implanted so deeply into people's psyche that they do not know the weapons are there and are used inadvertently against themselves. This is sometimes called religion.

Of course, to erase one's history literally is impossible. There is humour in this way of calling it, and it means to erase the effect on the present of all our past conditioning. To become a person of power and knowledge it is a prerequisite to erase one's conditioning and automatic behaviour, and to step outside the consensual reality agreement. To master the robot. This is a monumental task, not some New Age, five-minute-wonder cure. There are many levels of conditioning and the robot can be very subtly hidden within.

A wonderful example of this was a leaflet I received through the post recently from a New Age group who said they were 'lightworkers'. Page one was a eulogy about their wonderful work and how they were totally non-judgmental and way past all that sort of negativity. Page two was a vitriolic diatribe against another group of lightworkers who, they said, were channelling the 'wrong kind of light'. Whatever happened to self-awareness between pages one and two?

The task of undoing conditioning and freeing oneself from the bondage of personal history is called: stalking.

Regaining personal power through stalking

This is what much of this book is about. Stalking one's self to regain personal power and gain mastery over the robot. A good place to start looking is at addictions. Society's acceptable addictions are things such as smoking, drinking, sugar consumption, overeating/undereating, mind-numbing entertainments, co-dependent relationships, shopping, fashion, loveless sex, the lottery and meaningless trivia of all kinds. Anything to keep the mind busy so it does not think the kind of thoughts which might challenge the status quo. In other words, ways to keep from beginning the humbling journey of awakening. And it is a humbling journey.

Thieves in the night and day

The thing with addictions is that they are robbers. They rob you of your power, they have power over you which means you are losing power over yourself. An addicted person is a powerless person at the mercy of his/her desires, impulses and habits, a stimulus-response machine with little free will or mastery of self. The more you bring addictions to awareness and then under control of your will, the more power you will have over your life. Ask yourself now – Who is running my show? Who is running my life? In which areas am I really in charge and in which do I act like a robot? In which areas am I lived and in which do I live from my own volition? How much of my energy and my truth am I giving away to purchase what I perceive as my needs?

EXERCISE

List what feels like your areas of power loss and addictions. Make it a running list and then stalk yourself. Keep adding as you gain insight into what runs you and where you lose power, and deleting when you attain mastery.

The seven dark or 'shadow' arrows

Here is an excellent map to help the search. The dark or 'shadow' areas are:

1. Attachments
2. Dependencies
3. Judgments
4. Comparisons
5. Expectations
6. Neediness for approval
7. Self-importance

Areas 1 and 2: attachments and dependencies

Everything we are attached to and dependent upon that is not a necessity robs us of power. We can look at this the opposite way round and ask ourselves what is it we are *purchasing* by giving away power through 'attachment'. Typical attachments are about being accepted by others, parents, education, job–career, religion, cultural norms, the peer (beer) group, being seen as at a certain level of societal position, certain income etc., size of house, car, etc. We give away our power of free will and choice in order to purchase acceptance, approval, to belong, to feel 'in', to be fashionable, and so on. We sweat away working long hours to earn money to achieve status in order to feel okay. There is nothing on earth wrong with being accepted and approved of or to work hard or have nice things, the questions are: does it cost more than we realise and are we fully aware of our part in this transaction, i.e. are we acting consciously?

Look at what you are attached to and how this relates to your definition of self. If you are attached to youth and beauty, getting old will be tough. If you are attached to monetary wealth, status, your job and its description of your 'worth', you may suffer life's financial ups and downs. Attachments create pain when we lose whatever we have been attached to. We can call them 'pain games'.

Booze, ciggies, coffee, pharmaceuticals, drugs, gossip, co-dependent relationships, the I-love-you-can't-do-without-you/ I-hate-you-and-can't-stand-being-with-you syndrome, mindless trivia and so on are all escapes from reality when reality would hurt if we let it in. These are the pain games of dependency, they seem to keep the pain away but actually they are just the means by which we distract ourselves from facing the truth. They do no more than postpone the day of reckoning. Life catches up with us willy-nilly. The shamanic way is to face it now.

Attachments and dependencies are two aspects of the same area of pain games – fear of security, fear of being alone, fear of the unknown, fear of the future, fear of being without, fear of change. In trying to avoid life's pain, we give away monstrous amounts of power and free will in *purchasing* short term, apparent benefits from others and from life. In trying to keep pain at bay, we create it relentlessly by trying to protect ourselves from reality.

EXERCISE

List what you perceive as your attachments and dependencies.

◆ Put them in order of importance and then mark the ones you feel you can do something about right away.

◆ Select one and start work now.

Areas 3 and 4: judgments and comparisons

The judgments we make of others point to the areas we need to look at in ourselves. Judgments maintain isolation, loneliness and inner pain. Put-downs, fault finding, the see-saw effect of making oneself feel better by knocking others are just ways of bolstering a weak ego, and point to a reduced and hurting sense of self. When you listen to a really judgmental person ranting forth about the shortcomings of others, remember with compassion that they them-self are on the receiving end of that almost all their waking hours.

The healthy side of judgment is discernment, and we all need that to function. Not to judge does not mean to accept everything and everybody, such would be a nonsense. It is the negative energy of judging that hurts, the putting down of others to prop up a fragile ego.

Comparison is exemplified by the pecking order so beloved of ducks, and the collective group identity of 'us' versus 'them' and the ranking orders of hierarchies through which so much of society is organised. The question here is about looking consciously at what is being played out. We will always be ranked, compared, judged and so on, but by being aware we can play the role consciously without the pain game.

Of course I do realise if you are sufficiently advanced to be reading a book like this you will be way past judgments of all kinds. In fact you are probably amongst the top quartile of virtually enlightened people on the planet. Not that I myself am in any way judgmental of course, or comparative, especially about those poor unfortunates one might call ordinary people!

EXERCISE

♦ Take a look at 'those people' – the ones who you disapprove of – the ones you are better than. Consider all the things they do wrong that you do so much better. List them and their faults. Go on, have fun. Remember you are doing it in a non-judgmental way so it's okay. Isn't it?

Take a look at who and what you judge. Remember discernment is a vital ally in life. It is the judgmental put-downs we make about others where the hidden message is actually about making oneself feel better that hurt us. With real self-love and acceptance one does not have to put others down to feel better. Judgmentalness is rooted in lack of self-acceptance. This exercise can help you focus where you need to work.

Areas 5 and 6: expectations and neediness for approval

Expectation is about not being present. There is a lovely saying: 'Expect the unexpected without expectation.'

Not exactly an easy thing to do but a great spiritual practice. When we are not in the present, we are not really in life, we are in our heads. The only moment is now – now. I'll say it again – the only moment is now. Oh tish, now that one's gone too ... It is very difficult to harness the moment of now – the uncatchable moment – isn't it?

Much spiritual practice is about just that – learning to experience the moment of now. Fear is a tremendous motivator. Carlos Castaneda tells stories of how his teacher don Juan would frighten him so much to bring him fully to the present that he would defecate in his pants. This makes me think of *ayahuasca*, the shamanic medicine used in the Amazon jungle. Extreme perhaps, but effective.

Neediness for approval is what we all tend to suffer from when our ego – our sense of self – is fragile. When we feel needy we give away power to *purchase* approval, acceptance, 'love', inclusion and so on. Feeling power-less, we will come to feel angry deep inside but that, being seen as unacceptable and dis-approved, is likely to remain hidden and denied. Neediness is a common affliction and a great thief of power.

EXERCISES

Expectation: expect the unexpected without it.
The only moment is now. A good practice exercise for this is the urban vision quest (see Chapter 7).
Neediness: there are needs and there is neediness. We all have needs, that is human. But neediness has an energy about it that tends to drive away those who might help us fulfil our needs because it leaves little for others. It gives a feeling of I- me-me. All human needs are met reciprocally – you help me, I help you. A needy person radiates little energy to meet the needs of others so pushes away those who might meet his or her needs.

◆ Look at anywhere in life you feel unmet. Can you give a little more, take a little more to the exchange? Dare you give without conditions, i.e. without reward? That can be a tall order, but when the bank is empty, someone has to make the first deposit and it might as well be you.

Area 7: self-importance

Self-importance is the summation of the shadow arrows. They are all ways of being self-important, of seeing the world from the viewpoint of a damaged self, of looking to self before considering what and who is actually out there.

Self-importance brings great loneliness. It is accompanied by self-pity though that may tend to be less obvious. It includes not just pomposity but its opposite, shyness and inhibition. The shy person can be just as self-absorbed as the show-off – and just as lonely.

EXERCISE

◆ Look at any area in your life where you feel sorry for yourself. What triggers you into this feeling? Look at any area of shyness or where you feel inhibited. Who did you learn this from?

◆ With areas of shyness, take a look at how you can serve other people, or serve the situation. By focussing on what is needed from you, shyness can lessen and in time just disappear. After all shyness is only there when 'I' am there. When service is there instead of 'me', 'I' am not, so shyness is not.

EXERCISE

Just suppose your life was a movie . . . According to your age, a certain number of reels will have been completed but there is still much to go, the movie is by no means over. In your movie, you are the hero/heroine.

◆ What is the *main theme*?
   For example, finding your personal power and the right to live your life your way instead of just pleasing others. Or, battling chronic, low self-esteem learned from parents, and drowning it in alcohol. Or, desperately shy and inhibited, scared to speak up for yourself, walked on and downtrodden, rejected with no self-sense of worth, you struggle to make a place for yourself somewhere, somehow.

◆ What are the principal *stages* of your life? Name them.

◆ Are there *sub-plot dramas* that have tended to keep happening over and over?

◆ What kind of *petty tyrants* ('baddies') have had a habit of crossing your path and challenging you?

◆ Write a synopsis of the *movie of your life.*

◆ How has your life brought you to change?

◆ How have your political–spiritual views changed?

◆ What do you consider your successes and failures?

◆ How have you grown? Look for *main theme, life patterns, repetitive cycles.*

◆ Write the essence of the movie of your life as it is so far. Remember it is not finished. Look at the *direction* it is pointing . . .

◆ If you were to tell the *essence* of the story of your life so far in about 20 minutes, what events would encapsulate it best?

Reflect on what you learn from looking at your life like this. Look at where your life projects to if it continues on this path. Is this what you want for yourself? What you have written is a kind of hologram of your life – a segment which shows the pattern of the whole. What do you want to unfold in the remainder of the movie? Take the Eagle-eye, the 'sees far' view, and take a long look at the story of your life so far. Are there actions you could take now which will alter the course of your story and project it towards your desired goals?

Personality types

Now let us look at some basic personality types, ways we humans learn to compensate so we can get through somehow, ways we have learnt to survive through impossible times.

The placater, the distracter and the blamer

Harley Swiftdeer talked about these categories at a workshop I attended many years ago, and with his usual humour and forthrightness, he called them the Puke (placater), the Pisser (distracter) and the Fart (blamer). He said these categories come from Castaneda's don Juan and they are certainly blunt and unflattering enough to be. See if you recognise yourself – or parts of yourself, or people you know – in these descriptions.

The placater, or Puke, is a person who is so nice, so accommodating, so abjectly pleasing, so grovellingly accepting and accommodating of everyone and everything, so ready to agree to whatever you say and do that you are likely to end up wanting to puke all over him/her. The Puke is the pleaser, placater, do-gooder, super-nice person. The Puke feels terminally worthless and powerless. S/he suffers greatly from lack of self-esteem and thus desperately seeks approval, compares him/herself unfavourably, is submissive and highly dependent. But watch out for his/her judgments, so carefully hidden away so no one will really know what s/he thinks. S/he thinks very badly of him/herself and you can be sure that sooner or later s/he will think just as badly of you. Hang around him/her long enough and wait till s/he starts complaining and running people down, and you will know what is coming your way once you fail in the impossible task of being right for him/her all the time.

The distracter, or Pisser, is the space cadet, zombie, 'computer', distracter, never in the here–now, always away somewhere in the clouds or locked up with a computer screen, out of touch with feelings and emotions, looking way out into the future or back to the past, readily distracted, theorising about some abstract ideas ... I mean you can get seriously pissed off around a pisser. You can never get a hold of him or get a commitment out of him. He lives in definite-maybe-land, in expectation of the future, denial of the past, plays copiously at being unimportant. He dare not face his feelings of lack of self-worth so he tries not to face anything at all.

The blamer, or Fart, is the hostile person who attacks you before you even think of getting her. The Fart blames everything on someone and you just know there will be trouble if you step out of line – her line that is. The Fart looks at you and sees in you what she does not like about herself. She lives in self-importance with a nice dose of judgment and comparison to flavour the brew. She compensates for lack of self-worth with bravado and attempts at domination.

May I state my personal position on this, do you think? If I'm not taking up too much of your time that is, or using up too much paper. I mean you don't have to read this personal bit, you can just skip to the next paragraph. I mean – er–sorry! You see, I am (guess what) a Puke (in recovery) – but I also choose to be a Fart-in-training. In my early life I was a classic Puke and walked the world on eggshells, often feeling inside as if I should apologise for just existing. Hidden behind my bad posture and shrunken shoulders was a lot of repressed rage, and having no feeling of personal power I played it all out covertly. My self-esteem was at floor level if not somewhere under the carpet. Although most of that has long since gone out of my life, the idea of becoming a Fart-in-training is to reverse consciously those old instincts by affirming the opposite tendency. Not that I want to end up being a Fart, just a balanced human able to act out any personality mask I choose.

The latter is the fourth category, the spiritual warrior who has the freedom to act at will, with consciousness, in any situation.

EXERCISE

◆ **Part 1.** Watch yourself for the next 48 hours and see if you behave primarily like a Puke, Pisser or Fart when under stress. Check and monitor your automatic behaviour. How often do you behave like a warrior?

◆ Watch your inner dialogue and note down the gist of what you are telling yourself, especially at moments of stress.

◆ Carry a notebook with you and try to build into your day moments when you can check in with yourself and make notes. Hold the thought that you are stalking another being who lives inside you and does things that you, when fully conscious, would not necessarily do.

The automatic, domesticated, stimulus-response robot is a formidable part of each of us. By stalking you can get a handle on him/her and gradually gain power.

Exercise Part 2. From your notes elicit the essence of the messages you give yourself, the stories you are telling yourself.

Here is another way of looking at the same areas of personality and our weird and wonderful compensatory mechanisms. This time let's have fun with them.

Victim–persecutor–rescuer–rebel

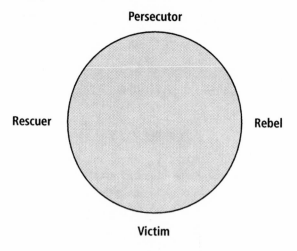

From victim to rebel

Feel yourself into these roles and see if one or more are familiar. Which roles do you tend to play and in relation to whom?

Victim. This is placater, or Puke, territory so you can go on till you feel sick. Poor You. When did you last feel martyred, victimised, put down, unfairly treated? The moment we resent others or complain, we are playing victim. To avoid it means taking responsibility for ourselves and our life. That is a tall order. Most of us have been brought up to blame and complain. Some people play victim and martyr a lot of the time and, perhaps, rather more than they would wish to admit. The great value in playing these as conscious roles is to bring awareness to them.

When playing victim, first of all think of all the circumstances which you could possibly interpret as being against you. Trains and buses which make you late, restaurants which overcharge, service which is slack. Then there are the people who have victimised you, parents who have made you what you are, bosses who made you work far too hard and paid you far too little, lovers who have taken what they wanted and then discarded you like an empty Coke bottle, children who want you to die so they can inherit your money, people who have pinched your best ideas and called them their own ... the list is endless. Get to feel really sad for yourself and fiendishly angry about all the frightful things *other people* are responsible for in your life. Take up the posture, the enfeebled voice, the bent neck, the weight on your shoulders, and *whinge*. (Have fun, it's only a role play ... isn't it?)

Persecutor. An aspect of the blamer, or Fart. Every victim needs a persecutor. Indeed every victim creates a persecutor, and vice-versa. Now it is time to find the farting persecutor inside you. Look at all these snivelling little victims, don't they deserve what they get? Wretched little people creeping about the world, moaning, complaining, whining, whingeing, fault-finding, boring you to death with their petty little concerns. Wouldn't you just like to tell them how pathetic and feeble they are? After all, how can any sensible person with any self-respect go through life like that? How can anyone with even a grain of intelligence be so utterly non-responsible for themselves? Ridiculous cringing little wets.

Find your posture and your walk as a persecutor, the position of your hands and the sound of your voice. If this role is unfamiliar, let yourself feel the feeling of covered-up powerlessness – yes, persecutors feel powerless too just like victims, but they handle it by aggression instead of whining – and remember that if you are going to get anywhere in the world, it will be by climbing over someone else's back. In this role, it is good to be bad. You can revel in those cutting remarks that you may have never dared to say in real life. You can creatively insult anyone if it will give you a moment's satisfaction. As a persecutor you need to make your mark so everyone will know you are not a person to be messed with. If there is anything going here, you are going to get your share first.

Rescuer. Sometimes we feel that we know best and can help others. We feel that we can do a good deed and rescue others from their own follies (and simultaneously earn a few credits in heaven). After all, poor unfortunate victims need someone to rescue them, don't they? And persecutors need to be helped to see that they don't need to behave badly. Yes, it's time to find the noble, self-sacrificing rescuer within.

Ask yourself how much good you can do by helping these poor unfortunate people to see the error of their ways, and what loving assistance you can give to those who seem over and over again to bring such suffering down upon their own heads. After all, you know better, don't you? You can help and advise, and the wise counsel that falls so easily from your lips will surely prevail. People will see sense when *you* get to show them just what a fountain of good sense *you* are. And those persecutors, they need to be told a thing or two, don't they? They think they are it, but you know it is all just bravado, just showing off. Furthermore, it's very mean to pick on those more helpless than oneself. They should pick on people their own size if they have to, not on poor unfortunates who are already victimised.

Find the posture of the saviour. Remember that you are there to save these poor people, whether they like it or not. *You* are the Robin Hood of emotional neuroses and *you* are going to bring them the riches of true self-knowledge. And, remember, if they don't like what you are doing, *you know best* and *you* can save them. After all, it is your vocation, and you know how good you are because you can count up how many you have saved already, as, naturally, you keep a record. So, let's hear some heroic martial music as you enter triumphantly like a white knight on a charger to the rescue.

Interestingly, it is the victim who potentially occupies the most powerful position of these three. The victim manipulates and controls and arranges his/her own martyrdom. A persecutor needs someone to persecute, a rescuer needs someone to rescue, but a victim can manage all on his/her own.

Although those are three interlocking archetypal roles, there is a fourth: the rebel. The real rebel is the one who attempts to find and take power over him/herself. To be a successful rebel one needs to take responsibility for one's actions. Without that, one is just making noise and is operating in one of the other categories. The rebel at his/her best is a spiritual warrior, and is making the passage out of this circle of neurotic interdependency, taking the courage to stop the game and take power and responsibility.

INDIVIDUAL EXERCISE

◆ Walk around and find one of the above characters within you. Start with the posture first, then walk, voice, phrase, expression, etc.

◆ Do this for each role.

◆ Identify which role you feel most at home with.

◆ Look at what has surfaced in the role-play.

GROUP EXERCISE

◆ Get everybody to walk around and find one of the four characters within themselves. Posture first, then walk, voice, phrase, expression, etc. Then interact with one or two other people playing their roles. Do this for each role.

- Then divide *ad hoc* into four subgroups, one group to play each role. Mingle and interact for a couple of minutes.

- Ask the participants to identify which role they feel most at home in. Next ask them to divide into four subgroups again, one for each role with the role now being their own choice. They then mingle again and interact.

- Then ask them what has surfaced for them in the role-play and discuss the issues.

- A subgroup becomes a panel and members of the groups ask them questions which they answer in role.

What may well happen in the role-play is that the roles change. The white knight rescuer may become a victim, the victim may easily start to persecute, the persecutor becomes rebel and the rebel may become a rescuer on the white charger. This kind of outcome can be very fruitful for understanding the dynamics.

A group exercise I learned from the Actors Institute which I really love and have had enormous fun with is this one:

GROUP EXERCISE

- Take the three roles: the placater–victim (oh poor me, help me, I need you, you must do something . . .), the blamer–persecutor (you snivelling little wet, do something for yourself you creep, you useless dungbeetle . . .) and the distracter–rescuer, giver of unconditional love and – useless – help (everything is wonderful, just listen to me and it will be all right, let me do it for you, I know best, I will save you, do shut up and listen to *me* . . .).

- Three people get up on 'stage' and perform each role simultaneously and totally for about 45 to 60 seconds only, then change roles until they have had a go at each character.

- Then three more get up and so on.

60

◆ The object is not to listen to the others but to present your role as virulently and forcefully as possible. The results are usually hilarious, and high energy is generated by playing out without restraint what is in all of us and remains generally repressed.

There are many more sophisticated models of personality types such as the Enneagram, a nine personality-types map based on the work of Gurdjieff, the Earth Medicine map in Kenneth Meadows's book of the same name, Ron Kurts's five body-structure types – to mention just three, but these basic maps I find profoundly useful.

Self-mythology

Now it is time for an exercise to elicit your own myths of yourself. I have conducted this exercise with many groups for over 14 years to help people uncover their mythologies and the gist always comes out the same. The fundamental personal negative myth of Western people is: I'm not good enough; I'm unworthy; I'm unlovable.

The basic challenge to people born in the West is lack of self-esteem, self-value, self-love, self-care. In addition it is very valuable to work at finding the more detailed personal myths and beliefs that lurk hidden in the psyche and exert their control without our realising it.

EXERCISE

Sit down quietly with your journal and reflect.

◆ Who/what pushes my buttons so I feel and act disempowered?

◆ What negative patterns seem to repeat themselves in my life?

◆ What are the deepest negative beliefs about myself that lurk within me? List the answers and take a good look. This is some of the 'hypnosis' that works away inside you. How much of it is actually true (if any) and how much is what your robot has learned from parents, siblings, peers etc. and repeats parrot fashion because that is all it knows?

♦ What are my deepest positive beliefs about myself? List them and reflect on yourself as a valued and loved part of Great Spirit.

Here are some typical myths of the personality types discussed.

Typical placater–victim myths:

I do not deserve so I feel guilty when I receive.

I want your approval and the only way I can get it is to hide my true self.

I am afraid to take my power/stand up for my rights because others will reject me if I do (i.e. I 'purchase' acceptance by giving away my power).

If I show who I really am I will be abandoned and rejected.

I am not good enough so I have to earn love.

I feel I must contribute to justify my presence.

I deal with other people's problems because mine are not worth dealing with.

If I become independent and strong, you [they] will not love me anymore.

It is not fair, however hard I try I am not going to get what I want.

I must never cause anyone any inconvenience.

I cannot get what I want because it is not fair to others if I do.

Typical distracter–rescuer myths:

Because I do not know what I want, I do not run the risk of not getting it.

If I show who I really am I will be abandoned and rejected.

I have got nothing important to say about myself because I am not important.

I cannot change it, decisions are made above me.

I feel stupid so I do not have to be self-responsible.

If I really connect to my feelings I will explode.

If I fully incarnate, something terrible will happen.
Typical blamer–persecutor myths:
I am more spiritually evolved so you will not understand me.
I am misunderstood and superior.
I have to work to support myself because no one else will.
All out attack is the best form of defence.
Everyone else can do it, they are all bastards anyway.
What the hell have I got to do for you to notice me?
At least I can be bloody good at being wrong.

Take a look and see which of them resonate with you. Are there any you have held true in the past? Are there any which feel as if they hold truth now? What have you learned about yourself?

Now you are ready for the Star Maiden's Circle.

The Star Maiden's Circle

Your life in reflection

I N THE GREAT WORK of 'erasing our personal history' or to put it less prosaically, healing our past traumas, the Star Maiden's Circle is a profound tool. It describes our human process in the form of a circle. By facing each direction in turn we gain illumination and understanding of life issues and a sense of compassion for our self in our life struggles.

The name Star Maiden's Circle comes from star: pure light of awareness; maiden: virginal, fresh; and circle: the place where two principles meet.

The Star Maiden's Circle is a circle both of the shadow – the unconscious parts of ourself, the old patterns of the automatic robot – and the light aspect of ourself who seeks liberation, freedom and truth.

The shadow circle is called the Circle of Foxes and it shows how, in our unconsciousness and unawareness, we chase our own tail and create a mire of our own making. On the light side, the Dance of the Coyotes teaches us how to seize the chance to shift our consciousness, take responsibility for our predicament and change our circumstances. This latter is the path of the hero/ine who walks the mythological hero's journey challenging demons, fighting dark forces and conquering for the good of all at whatever risk to self.

The Star Maiden's Circle

Each direction is a point of view

The world from that view is either revealed to us as it is – which means we see it in light, the pure light of awareness, lit up, clear and understandable – or we see only dark, in shadow, because we have become trapped in fixation, and all is unclear, muddy, and seems to be full of pitfalls and traps.

Now it is time to embark on a hero/ine's adventure into the healing of personal history using this wonderful all-encompassing medicine-wheel teaching, but first of all here is an exercise to do outside in nature.

EXERCISE: THE CEREMONY

Ceremonial exercise based on the Star Maiden's Circle. Flowering tree ceremony for understanding the inner child.

◆ Find a tree, any tree that feels good and welcomes you, and find four stones, one for each direction.

◆ Be aware not only of your inner landscape but of signals and intimations from Mother Nature. A cloud formation, a bird, a movement in the grass. Allow that Mother Nature speaks to you. It is just that we have forgotten that nature is alive and communicates with us all the time, and so most of us do not hear many of her messages. Put yourself in as receptive a mode as you can without expectation. Just be there.

◆ Take something to offer, e.g. tobacco, rice, chocolate, and your journal.

◆ Create and empower your own circle around the tree. Lay your stones in the cardinal directions. When you are ready, begin the ceremony. Make your offering and call the spirits, sitting with your back to the tree:

– Face south and ask, 'How does my inner child feel and see the world?'
– Face north and ask, 'How does the everyday adult me feel and experience the world?'
– Face west and ask, 'How does the priest/ess within me feel and sense the world?'
– Face east and ask, 'How does the magical child within me feel and see the world?'

◆ Now work the non-cardinal points of the wheel. These are the 'movers'. With your back to the tree:

– Face south-west and ask, 'What are the dreams I wish to manifest? What do I wish to create and giveaway to the people?'
– Face north-west and ask, 'What are the rules and laws I make for myself? Do they support and nurture or limit me?'

- Face north-east and ask, 'How do I choreograph my life? How do I make my choices and do those choices bring me the dreams I seek?
- Face south-east and ask, 'How do I feel about myself deep inside? How do I see myself?'

◆ Notice what is occurring both in and around you at all times. Watch to see if the outer world mirrors the inner world.

◆ When you have finished, clear away your stones and any signs of your presence. Offer something to the tree again, and give thanks.

Tree ceremonies are good to do regularly. They are a great tool for checking in with your inner self and gaining insight.

EXERCISE: STAR MAIDEN'S CIRCLE

◆ Arrange a circle with eight points according to the compass directions, with room for you to sit in the centre. You might like to mark the cardinal points – for example with a candle at the east, a cup of water at the south, a little earth at the west and perhaps a feather or something to indicate wind at the north. Make yourself a comfortable place in the centre and sit down there with your notebook.

◆ *Face south* and contemplate the question, 'How was I wounded?' The subtext is how was I patterned, trained, made to fear, inhibited, restricted, set against myself and so on? How was my inner robot developed? From the exercises we have done before, this information should be quite readily available.
Write down what comes without censoring in any way.

◆ *Face north* and answer the question, 'How is life for me today?' The wounding which is still working away in my life is likely to show itself in my everyday experience. My inner robot will be trying to keep my show on the road in the habitual way it knows, the way it is patterned to do so.
Write down what is working and what is not working in everyday life.

◆ *Face west* and answer these questions, 'How do I feel about my body? How much do I feel connected to my body? Does it feel like "me" or something I just live in? How do I treat my body? Do I keep myself fit and healthy, is that a priority? Do I feed it with good food and neither too much nor too little? To what extent am I in charge of my body or is my body in charge of me?'
Make a list of any changes you may find you would benefit from making.

◆ *Face east* and answer these questions, 'Does my magical child get to play? Do I have happy times, perhaps with children, just for fun? How are my sexual experiences? Are they times when I can be the magical child in the grotto of delights? Or are they something else? If something else, what old automatic behaviour, what conditioning, what fear and what old voices are in there with me screwing up the beauty that could be?'
List what comes to mind.

The shadow aspects

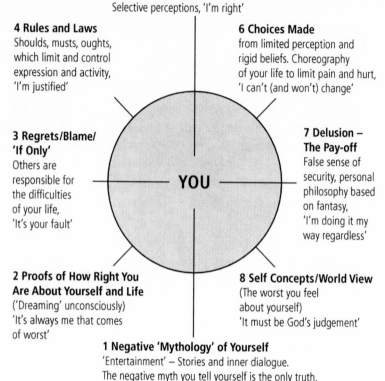

5 Limiting Beliefs about Yourself
and the scope of your life.
Selective perceptions, 'I'm right'

4 Rules and Laws
Shoulds, musts, oughts,
which limit and control
expression and activity,
'I'm justified'

6 Choices Made
from limited perception and
rigid beliefs. Choreography
of your life to limit pain and hurt,
'I can't (and won't) change'

**3 Regrets/Blame/
'If Only'**
Others are
responsible for
the difficulties
of your life,
'It's your fault'

YOU

**7 Delusion –
The Pay-off**
False sense of
security, personal
philosophy based
on fantasy,
'I'm doing it my
way regardless'

**2 Proofs of How Right You
Are About Yourself and Life**
('Dreaming' unconsciously)
'It's always me that comes
of worst'

8 Self Concepts/World View
(The worst you feel
about yourself)
'It must be God's judgement'

1 Negative 'Mythology' of Yourself
'Entertainment' – Stories and inner dialogue.
The negative myth you tell yourself is the only truth,
'Poor me, I'm the victim'

The shadow aspects – the Circle of Foxes

EXERCISE CONTINUED

Now return to face the south once again. The story I tell myself:

The 'shadow' aspects of this direction are all the ways we sabotage ourselves, the stories we tell ourselves of worthlessness and unlovability, addictions we succumb to, the buried 'demons' – the traumas which cause unconscious reactions in us and bring havoc to our lives. These emanate mainly from negative childhood and adolescent experiences and fester within bringing misery and unhappiness. They can even bring physical illness until such time as we shine the light of consciousness on our inner self to clear the effects of these memories, to 'erase personal history'.

◆ This time the question is, 'What are or have been my personal mythologies, the stories I have told myself of who I am, and what permission I have to live?'

Here are a few subsidiary questions to reflect upon:

1. What childhood traumas/dramas still seem to govern my life?

2. What was I taught to fear when I was a child?

3. What did my parents and teachers want me to become/to do in life (and not to become and not to do)?

4. What anger, shame, guilt, bitterness do I still hold on to?

5. Who (what, where) do I still seek acceptance from?

6. What sort of things do I need to happen to make me feel okay?

7. What was my teenage life about, what was my drama in those years?

◆ Go back to the work we did earlier on personal mythology and on personality types. List the base-line inner stories you tell yourself.

◆ On a scale of one to ten, what is your level of self-esteem/self-worth?

◆ On a scale of one to ten, what is your typical level of emotional fear in everyday situations?

Face south-west. Wishing and hoping ... and being right:

This direction is about our dreams, wishes, hopes, all that we seek to make manifest in the world, and also the world's reflected 'dream' that comes back towards us. In other words what the world shows us by way of response. For example the person who says, 'Oh that always happens to me, if there is anything nasty flying around it's always my head it drops on', or perhaps one day you get out of 'the right side' of bed on what feels like a good day, and the world reflects that to you, and things go along just fine. Another day you get out of 'the wrong side of bed' and everything in sight goes wrong, is out of step, or is awkward and difficult. The fact that the cornerstone is your attitude on getting out of bed is wholly lost in the day-to-day adventure of life.

Here are a few quotations from some who knew the power of the dream:

'We are what we think, all that arises with our thoughts.' (*Buddha*)

'A man's life is what his thoughts make of it.' (*Marcus Aurelius*)

'As a man thinketh in his heart so is he.' (*Proverbs 23.7*)

'You become what you think about.' (*Earl Nightingale*)

'As you believe so shall it be.' (*Jesus*)

'With our thoughts we make the world.' (*Buddha*)

'The ancestor of every action is a thought.' (*Emerson*)

'Whether you think you can, or whether you think you can't, you're right.' (*Henry Ford*)

> Sow a thought, reap an action
> sow an action, reap a habit
> sow a habit, reap a character
> sow a character, reap a destiny. (*Ancient Chinese Proverb*)

Look at it this way: we are 'dreamers' all the time, consciously or not. Our current life, from this point of view, is a result of all our 'dreaming' to date. If you do not like anything about your life, you had a hand in 'dreaming' it and thus manifesting it into reality.

Questions to look at:

◆ What is life reflecting to you about your life? What is it showing you that works and what doesn't work. Look at your attitudes in all matters both obvious and, as far as you can delve into, hidden. Here are some questions to help:

1. What is despicable to you? What are you really afraid of doing?

2. What kinds of people and what situations do you avoid like the plague?

3. Do you have any bad dreams or nightmares?

4. What are your certainties – what are you absolutely sure about?

5. How do you stop yourself doing what you really want to do that you fear others may disapprove of?

◆ List what you have found out.

Face west. Broken dreams:

The west, this first time around, is the place of broken dreams, of regrets, of 'if onlys' and of blame for those who seemed to get in your way and stop you manifesting your dream-life. Feel into the place of 'if-only'. Let yourself go to that place of regret and blame, and note what comes up. Perhaps some tears come, that's good, perhaps some sore feelings are revisited, some hurts and pains. This is all trapped life force that can be set free. Like healing a physical wound, we have to clean out the pus before the healing will really happen.

◆ Helpful questions to ask yourself:

1. Who and what is to blame for my life?

2. What and who do I hold on to for security?

3. What am I most afraid of changing? What do I cling to?

4. What seems to limit me economically?

5. How good is my physical health and vitality?

6. In what areas did my parents tell me that I must succeed or am bound to fail?

◆ Make a list of what you feel ready to let go of, broken dreams that can be released, angry feelings that are perhaps now redundant and pointless. You might care to make an artifact to represent these feelings, perhaps out of natural things from the garden, or out of paper and crayons, or perhaps just a written list will suffice. What works for you is what is right.

Now face north-west. Justification:

This direction is about the ultimate justice of the universe and therefore about the action of karma in our lives. To accept one's karma means to accept the lessons we are here to learn and which life serves up to us. Karma means actions bringing reaction. What you do brings results, the question is: is it the result you want?

North-west relates to the making of rules and the robot-self loves that. Are you limiting yourself by making rules for yourself based on past experience, or are you creatively daring to make new rules which support you in your life today? The negative rules are those we make for ourselves by which we govern, bind and limit our lives, our creativity, our rights, our sexual expression and so on, and keep old pain-games and self-negating beliefs going.

◆ Here are helpful questions to consider:

1. What must, should, ought I do and not do?

2. What do I most fear will happen if I do not fulfil the above rules?

3. What is responsible for limiting me?

4. What would I absolutely, categorically and under any circumstances never do?

◆ Look at the rules and laws you make for yourself. What do you allow and not allow yourself to do? Especially look at the sacred cows of your life. When you live out your mythology (south) what do you have to disallow from your life to keep those stories going? The feeling of being wounded demands that some areas of life are not looked at. See if you can discern what those no-go areas are.

Face north. Bullshit or knowledge?

North is the mind, the wind, the everyday adult aspect of us. We visited before and asked how life is today. This time around we need to look at belief systems, about our programmes which control how we think. It could be framed as the 'rules and laws of our permitted thinking'. This is where conditioning is closest to brainwashing because the mind we use to think this through is the same one that went through the conditioning process to learn how to betray its truth and become an acceptable domesticated adult.

◆ If you have travelled abroad long enough to have culture shock on return, list what you can remember of how your culture looked and felt before you were re-integrated.

◆ Take a look at your beliefs of the 'sort of person', you believe you are. You will probably find a great deal of good in your list. That is not the point, the point is that this is someone you have learned to become. Knowing yourself starts with knowing what your programme is so you can go on from there.

◆ Here are more helpful questions:

1. Who and what do I secretly desire to take revenge upon?

2. When do I/what makes me lose my sense of humour?

3. What seems to cause me to lose my focus and my clarity of purpose?

4. What am I closed minded about, and addicted to?

5. People are .../life is ... What fixed beliefs do I hold?

6. What do I do/how do I manipulate to gain recognition?

Face north-east. Choice:

The place of choice, of design and choreography of energy. Are you making choices based on past pain and trauma, and with a fantasy idea of the future? Or are you able to make your choices freely from where you actually are now for your greatest happiness and the greatest good? How often do you live easily in a relaxed way, achieving maximum effect with minimum effort? Or do you seem to have to struggle like crazy to get anything much done at all? How much do you feel at the mercy of others, of your life circumstances? To what extent do you really take responsibility for yourself and your life?

♦ Look at how you make your choices in life. Choice – north-east – is between mind (north) and spirit (east). Do you make up your mind after reasoning only? Or do you touch into spirit and feel what is moving there. What inspiration can you sense to illuminate your choices?

♦ More questions to ask yourself:

1. What decisions do I tend to make based on avoiding a repeat of past pain and trauma?

2. What decisions do I tend to make based on a fantasy idea of the future?

3. What am I fanatical about and make unquestioning decisions to do/not do?

4. When and how am I moved around against my will by others?

5. When do I often seem to exert lots of effort for little gain?

Now face east. Point of reckoning:

This direction is about where we reap what we have sown. How we have chosen to mythologise, dream, and lead our life brings us to the point of reckoning. This is where the pay-off comes for all that has taken place so far around the wheel. We reap what we sow in either illumination and a gaining of more power over our self and our quality of life, or in delusion, confusion and grief. Let's go quickly around the wheel in reverse and see more of how this works:

The shadow circle means that I reap delusion, and confusion (east) – but with a sense of (false) security – as the result of frightened choices (north-east), mental bullshit and avoidance of facing issues (north), self-limiting rules (north-west), blame and regret (west), self-negating dreaming (south-west) and 'poor me' mythologies (south). The pay-off is that I do not have to face myself, take responsibility for my life and deal with the consequences that will entail.

So now facing the east, ask yourself what you are reaping in your life. To what extent are you manifesting dreams that you desire or dreams that you do not want. Look at how much of your outer behaviour and inner dreaming are automatic and governed by stimulus-response mechanisms and are products of conditioning.

◆ Ask yourself these questions:

1. What brings up feelings of hopelessness in me?

2. Are there areas where I am still controlled by religion?

3. When and to whom do I tend to present my life as better than it really is, i.e. lie to myself and others?

4. When do I tend to live my life for someone else?

5. When and how do I tend to get burnt out?

6. What do I get out of living my life this way?

Face southeast. Poor me:

The final direction relates to our self-concepts – how we feel about ourselves at our deepest core. When we live according to our shadow, limiting and protecting our self from life, we have little self-worth and feel pretty lousy inside.

◆ Ask yourself:

1. When am I the victim of life? When do I persecute others?

2. When do I give up my real self to fit in, gain approval?

3. How much of my real self is lost in the struggle to get by?

The final question is simply this. On a dark night, when you are alone, quiet, and there is no outside stimulus, no ego support, nothing external to feel good about, how do you in your deepest inner place feel about yourself?

The light aspects

Now it is time to go around the wheel from the light point of view and see what can be changed.

5 Alignment with Inner Knowing
Balance and harmony in the mind,
'I seek knowledge and wisdom'

4 Life-affirmative Rules and Laws
created by your own conscious
volition. Awareness of Sacred Law.
'I am in the world but not of it'

**6 Choices Made with
Guidance of Spirit**
for highest good, 'I am
at cause in my life'

**3 Taking full
Responsibility**
for yourself and
your life. No
blame, 'Dancing
the dream awake,'
'I am responsible
for myself and my life'

YOU

**7 Illumination/
Understanding**
The joyful pay-off
for living in
beauty, 'I follow
my bliss'

2 Conscious 'Dreaming'
of the life you desire. Openness to
all possibilities, 'I am open to try
anything and willing to learn
from mistakes'

8 Self Concepts/World View
Honouring and loving your self,
'I honour myself as an aspect of
Great Spirit'

1 Re-inventing/Re-mythologising Your Self
Becoming/being who you choose to be,
'I can become who and what I want'

The light aspects – the Dance of the Coyotes

78

EXERCISE

Face south again. My innate worth:

Now the task is to re-mythologise yourself. Suppose you had been 'born in blessing' with no concept of 'born in sin'. Suppose you had grown up and been taught of your innate goodness, your full entitlement to be a member of the family, tribe, village, town, city where you lived. Suppose you had been taught of spirituality as belonging, a connection to All-That-Is, and of your unique value to the people and the contribution you were needed to make for the good of the collective.

◆ Take a moment now to affirm yourself, your innate goodness, your unique value, your right to exist as part of the universe, your oneness with All-That-Is. Breathe this feeling in, savour this truth. Then when you are ready, tell yourself stories about yourself from that perspective, who you are, why you are here, and what you have to do and what is your unique giveaway for the benefit of Mother Earth and her people?

◆ Write it down. See the difference from the old stories.

◆ Here are helpful questions to ask yourself:

    1. What makes me feel really alive and full of vitality?

    2. What brings me feelings of harmony, balance and joy?

    3. What knowledge do I seek for my growth and well-being?

    4. Who and what do I really trust?

    5. What do I have to offer for the benefit of others?

Face south-west. Re-dreaming yourself:

Now is the time to look back into the 'dream' of your life and re-dream yourself. This time from the new feeling about yourself, let yourself dream of how you truly wish to make it become, the life you truly wish to manifest. Leave rationalisation, old beliefs of human limitation and so on at the door; never mind how long it might seem to take, or how practical it is in the so-called 'real world'.

◆ Write your dreams of the life you really want to bring into being. Let yourself go unrestrictedly, be electrified, let the paper you write on glow and shine.

◆ Helpful questions to stimulate you:

  1. What new adventures do I wish to engage in?

  2. What do I wish to explore freely and shamelessly?

  3. What dreams do I seek to actualise?

  4. What kinds of people am I really drawn to?

Face west. Action in beauty:

Now is the time to get practical and look at what you can do now in order to open the way for your dreams to be manifested. First practical steps: boldness. This is where trust, faith, comes in. Trust in the universe, trust that the universe will support you when you put your whole self into something. Another way of putting this is to say that energy follows thought. Or that intent and focus are what creates action.

◆ List the practical steps you can now take towards achieving your goals. Put your list up on a wall where it is going to catch your eye frequently and keep reminding you of what you wish to do.

◆ Helpful prods:

  1. How much do I feel aligned to the Earth?

  2. Where, how and with whom dare I let myself be my real self?

  3. How often and how much am I in the here and now?

  4. How is my physical health and vitality?

  5. Am I letting death be my advisor rather than my enemy?

Facing north-west. Sacred rule and law:

Now it is time to review those rules and laws, judgments, shoulds, musts and oughts, that you used to make for yourself, and to rewrite them.

◆ What rules will support you and guide you helpfully without unnecessary restriction? You are in command of your life, so what works for you?

◆ Make a new list of what guidelines are helpful.

◆ Ask these questions:

1. What is sacred to me?

2. When is my timing synchronous, effortless and in tune with the universe?

3. What brings a feeling of beauty into my life?

Face north. Knowledge and wisdom:

The light of the north is that elusive quality of instinctual 'knowing', of being in alignment with spirit, in balance with the forces of the cosmos, in harmony with the way things are intended to be, in the present moment and not out there trying to make things fit a plan of ego. Culture and language are a web of agreed-upon notions developed over generations by tacit agreement through which we are taught to perceive and which we learn to use to communicate with others. Wisdom is knowing that's all they are, bullshit is believing that's how it really is.

◆ Facing north look again at your belief systems and things you have taken for granted just because that was what you had been taught to believe. What do you now see that is in fact not true and not helpful and that can be ditched? What constitutes inner knowledge and is a certain and solid foundation for you in life? Some things that were once beliefs now may appear conjecture. Not necessarily wrong, but no longer certainties. That's okay, they can simply be placed in the category of definite maybes. Now you know they are not certainties, you can take an adventurous attitude and be open to learn what really is so.

◆ Take a look at these questions:

1. What really gives my life meaning and pleasure?

2. How/when do I co-ordinate my efforts and succeed?

3. What successes have I had and what skills have I mastered?

4. What philosophies make sense to me now and nurture my spirit?

5. What is true for me now as I look at the world and my life with fresh eyes?

Face northeast. Conscious choice:

Now you come back to choice. You looked at how you made choices before. Now, knowing that you have full responsibility for the outcomes and that no one else is responsible but you, how will you choose to make your choices? The proverbial buck stops here. It is your life and you are the only one who can become master of it. Others will have tried to master you but they had no business doing so; all the conditioning you received has put other voices in there, other patterns that were not yours. Now it is time to live making consciously chosen choices and to learn from the outcomes – the universe teaches us all through the action of karma.

◆ Ask yourself these questions:

1. On what occasions do I master my life and achieve the results I seek?

2. When and how do I achieve maximum effect with minimum effort?

3. When do I take responsibility for myself and express natural leadership?

East. Path-with-heart:

◆ Face the east and ask yourself what is the pay-off now for living my life this way. How does the reconfiguration of the energy of my life affect the outcome.

◆ Your questions:

1. When do I act clearly from my position of free-will choice?

2. When and how do I best express my artistic originality?

3. When and how do I naturally express my full potential?

4. When and how do I bring beauty into the world for the benefit of others?

5. When do I touch the freedom and joy of the magical child?

6. When does my joyful and loving magical child dance me?

7. What is my true path-with-heart? What is my give-away?

South-east. Spiritual warrior:

Lastly, how does this circle leave me feeling about myself?

◆ Ask yourself:

1. When am I a spiritual warrior living my truth?

2. When do I live my truth and take full responsibility for doing so?

3. When do I dare to enter the unknown with confidence? ('Feel the fear and do it anyway')

4. When am I part of the solution and no longer part of the problem?

Now let us go around this circle backwards and review its meaning:

The light aspect of the east means I reap illumination, 'seeing'. This comes from healthy life-affirmative and courageous choices (north-east), following a sense of knowing (north), through trancendence of my old robotic rules for myself and my life (north-west), a greater acceptance of responsibility for my situation (west), through dreaming a positive dream of my real deep desires for the kind of life I wish to live (south-west), which I can do after re-mythologising myself as a person of worth and value (south).

Finally, look at the two circles, two ways of being, two maps of yourself and your possibilities, two 'dreams' of the life you can manifest. What do you learn from this?

Sexuality

In earlier chapters we have mentioned sexuality and the negative beliefs and mind-control which have been so powerfully placed around this area of human life. It is such a fundamental area in which so much energy naturally resides. It has been the target of such an extraordinary amount of self-negation, denial, denigration of woman and the Earth, splitting off, flagellation, self-flagellation and self-immolation, all of which lurks in the hidden collective memory and does enormous damage to the potential of us living a loving life, that it deserves extra attention.

Just consider for a moment the words commonly used for the act of sex and our sexual organs. One way the sexual act is commonly described is as a fuck. The origin of that word is interesting. In the eighteenth century and possibly earlier, when adultery was a crime, people were jailed 'For Unlawful Carnal Knowledge', which abbreviates to F.U.C.K. Apparently this abbreviation was commonly put outside their cell to identify the reason for incarceration. Other common expressions are screw, bonk, make out, get your end away, have it off, get your leg over. The words most used for the male organ are cock, willy, dick, tool, and for the female the horrible word cunt, or hole. There is not a single positive, beautiful, affimative, loving, expression among them. Every single word or expression in common English usage is in at least some way derogatory. That speaks volumes about our collective attitude to sex, and we have inherited this from our past, our ancestors. I know too what will happen if I suggest some loving words instead. Along will come 'tabloid consciousness' and make fun of them so as to ensure we keep to these negative, downgrading, down-putting, stultifying attitudes.

In the Cherokee language, the male organ is a *tipili* and the female a *tupuli*. In Hindu it is *yoni* and *vajra*. The act itself is potentially the most creative act any of us can do because that is how we continue our species, it is how we all get born, it is the nearest to Divine creation we can get. It is also potentially the most beautiful of experiences, although we all know it can be anything else as well. It is in essence an act of Divine love and creation, yet practically our whole culture speaks of it degradingly at every opportunity.

Then there is menstruation. The great blessing of the blood of potential creation is often called the curse. In many old cultures it was considered a great blessing. Native American women would go to the Moon Lodge for the three days of bleeding to rest and renew themselves in peace and quiet. Nowadays women are expected to carry on regardless with the aid of Tampax. This is not in tune with the bodily rhythm of the female human. There is potential for enormous constructive cultural change here.

Now let us go around the Star Maiden's Circle again from a sexual point of view. This may be quite a challenging exercise to do, so be sure to choose a good moment when you can have plenty of quiet time for yourself.

Set up the circle as before and, when you feel ready, sit again in the centre and face the north. This time we will start from the point of view of the adult persona.

EXERCISE

Face north

+ Pose the question: how is your sex life now? Is it a regular visit to the magic grotto of sensual and loving delights? Does my body take me on a trip down Ecstasy Lane? Is it a time of losing ego control in a delightful way and allowing nature (God) to do what comes naturally? Is it share and share alike with your partner, and do you both find your way to ecstasy?

+ Or is it something else? A closed-hearted struggle to get some pleasure out of a rather boring and trying situation? Hopes dashed as things fail to work out the way you desired and you feel rejected, half-loved or just tolerated at best? Or is it a struggle to find partners, and do you get bored easily? Does your lovemaking become repetitive and deadening so you constantly seek new partners for excitement? How is it for you?

♦ Write it truthfully in your journal. No one else is going to read it, you can be brutally honest with yourself. Honesty is the thing that pays in the end.

Face south

♦ Face your wounded place. How were you wounded sexually? Were you rejected as a boy/girl early in life? What happened to you that hurt your very tender blossoming sexuality? Or were you supported at that time? What happened at puberty? Was your burgeoning sexuality welcomed by your family. If you are a woman, were you taught about menses and helped to adapt to the natural changes in your body? If you are a man, were you guided in what to do with the portion of yourself that had extended into a new, powerful and mysterious organ, taught of its beauty, told what it is for and how it can bring joy? How were your teenage years and what was your experience of those dances or social gatherings of that time?

Face west

♦ How does your body feel in sex? How much do you feel in touch with the physical and with your nature? How much does your body lead you in the act of sex and reveal itself to you? How much are you able to feel the opposite gender polarity in you?

Face east

♦ How much are you in touch with your magical child in sex? How much of sex is magical for you? Does sex take you into the realm of timelessness and effortless delight-in-being? During and after orgasm, do you find your consciousness is lifted to a place of inner silence and delight?

Now return to the south of your wheel:

♦ What are your deepest myths and beliefs about yourself as a sexual being? Forget any bravado, what is the truth? What do you really hold as truth about the sexual you?

Face south-west
♦ What are your sexual dreams, the scenarios that you put up on your mind-screen that make the best masturbation? (If you have never done that, you are definitely unusual.) How would you really like your sex life to be? What would bring you the greatest delights? What sexual dreams do you wish to make real?

Face west
♦ Do you have unfulfilled dreams, regrets? What never seems to be quite right for you? Do you feel frustrated, let down? What does the 'if only . . .' voice say?

Face north-west
♦ What rules govern your expression of sexuality? What limits do you put on yourself? What dare you never do? What dare you not ask a partner to do with you? What would horrify you if your partner asked you to do it? What patterns replay themselves in your lovemaking and with your partners?

Face north
♦ What are your beliefs about sex? What is your philosophy about sex and its expression? How should sex be conducted? Is it spiritual for you or is it devoid of spirituality? What do you believe sex is really about and what is it for?

Face north-east
♦ How do you choose your partners and your sexual experiences? Do the experiences you have seem to follow the choices you make? How do you choreograph your sexual experiences?

Face east

◆ What is the pay-off from your choices? To what extent do you feel your lovemaking is connected with spirit?

Face south-east

◆ How do you feel about yourself as a sexual being?

Re-framing and re-mythologising sexuality into beauty and joy

Tantra is about the full creative spiritual divine expression of sexuality. There is a native American teaching which is similar called *Quodoushka*. These ancient pre-Christian ways are about integrating sexuality and spirituality and raising our life-force energy. In other words about gaining personal power. Most of us Westerners have a monumental inner task to do to release the centuries of dogmatic denigration of sexuality and of its association with dirt and filth and to bring it into consciousness as the beauty, joy, love, and energy-raising stimulation that it is. There is the old saying: 'you can't make love and war'. But if your loving is unsatisfactory and your sex brings only half-baked pleasure and it does not raise your energy properly but instead drains you, then making war can seem like an alternative. Largely unconsciously, of course – but it is unhappy people who make wars, who feel they need other people's land and property, who feel the need to dominate and control. Happy people do not need to do these things. Look at yourself and your own life, at the times you have been happy and contented and the things you have spent your time doing at these times. Then look at the times you have been unhappy, disconnected and alone, and the things you have done at those times.

Sex, after all, is how we were all born, it is how life goes on. If that is not spiritual, what is? It seems that most animals have no orgasmic responses to sex, only us humans and one or two other species like dolphins have that. So the Creator creates humans in this way, and incredibly stupid humans declare war on their own sexuality and its natural God-intended pleasure and make centuries of misery and repression. If that isn't just plain asinine stupidity, what is? We have the power to recover from this lunacy but each one of us has to do it for our self.

EXERCISE

Reframe your self as a being of innate worth, of valued and beautiful sexuality, born in blessing and out of joy. Reframe sexuality itself as a deep expression of spirit. A path of loving, sharing and giving to another, to others, of the highest creativity in life.

- *Facing south:* it is time to re-mythologise yourself, create a new story for yourself of beauty, joy and power in your natural expression of your sexual being. It is time to claim your sexual self in its fullness and potency, in its ability to bring joy and happiness, in its creative drive for union with another.

- *Facing south-west:* Look at your dreams of what you really want to call into your life which will bring a feeling of sustained and sustainable happiness and satisfaction. What will bring you the greatest sensual, sexual, bodily, spiritual, energetic delight and joys. What dreams will bring you the greatest feelings of innate worth and beauty in the full expression of your humanity?

- *Facing west:* action. What steps can you take to manifest your dreams into everyday reality?

- *Facing north-west:* new rules and laws for the conduct of your sex life as an expression of your truth, in beauty and joy.

- *Facing north:* it is time to release any old negative beliefs about sex that no longer serve you and to replace them with life-affirmative concepts based on the natural innate rightness of sexuality as a divine part of life.

♦ *Facing north-east:* now you get to review and renew your choices. What sort of sexual partner(s) will bring you the greatest long-term life-affirmative happiness and joy? What kind of relationship(s) will bring that to you? What sexual choices are completely in tune with your being and the deeper purposes of your life as you now see them?

♦ *Facing east:* what is the pay-off for this circle of life? How does it feel to unite your sexual expression with your spiritual being?

♦ *Facing south-east:* how do you feel about yourself now?

Complete your ceremony and give thanks. Then take some time to really look at what has been revealed and what you have learned.

There is one more very important issue to add to this:

Puberty rites

One of the saddest omissions from life in the Western World is the loss of puberty rites. I remember a friend a 60-year-old woman – lamenting the frightfulness of her 80-year-old mother and telling me awful stories of her mother's lack of caring and concern. As I attempted to guide her towards taking her power back and owning her own life, she burst out, 'But I want my mummy!' She was not a client so I had no real permission to confront her with herself and she made it clear there was not much I could do to help. That is just one story but in my practice I constantly find people of all ages bound to their parents' thinking, and sometimes even more literally to their parents, in ways that are not at all healthy. Most often it is purely in their emotions, not even in external life such as family and money. They just haven't taken themselves on and are still tied to or blaming parents, or mouthing off parental injunctions of old as if they are still being pushed around. Sadly it is only reasonable – they never went through puberty rites to break the ties so they are still tied.

Last year my colleagues Dawn Russell, Andy Raven and I had the opportunity to take 16 people between the ages of 25 and 53 through puberty rites. We created the rite based on the medicine-wheel teachings with which, as a template, one can create almost anything and be alchemically correct. It is written here so that you can do this yourself. This is the preparation phase.

EXERCISE

Go out into nature, find a sitting place and face each of the cardinal directions in turn. Find five stones, one for each direction and one for the centre.

- Face the west and ask, 'what power of mine does my mother still hold?'

- Face the east and ask, 'what power of mine does my father still hold?'

- Face the south and ask, 'what power of mine do any of my siblings hold [or anyone similar if no siblings]?'

- Face the north and ask, 'what power of mine do any of my peers still hold?'

- Face the centre and ask for blessings and to be shown how you gave power away.

- Give thanks.

- Then sit alone and meditate, ask, 'am I really ready to take my power back and take full responsibility for my life and my self?' That means no one to blame, to place responsibility on no one else, no one to be an adult while I behave like a child, no more self-pity.

Do not proceed further until you can answer with a very affirmative yes.

Our ceremony had two parts, each being held in a separate room. For the first each participant chose four others to represent for them his/her mother, father, sibling and peer. Then we convened in a small circle with the participant in the centre. S/he gave to each of the four holders of the directions the stone symbolising the power s/he desired to claim back. The fifth stone was passed through to the second part of the ceremony.

EXERCISE

Sit in a comfortable place with space all around you and place your four cardinal stones in the four directions, keeping the centre stone with you. Visualise in turn each of the four people/energies and 'see' whatever power you feel they may still hold that is yours. Get really clear on what that power is and how much you want it back.

In the second part of our ceremony, each participant, without knowing what was coming, was led into the next room and found themselves facing the representatives of mother, father, siblings and peers, who were standing one behind the other. They then declared, first to the mother, the power that they demanded back. Only when the person representing mother felt that it was really meant and was not pleading but coming from a place of power, did they hand over the stone. This progressed to all four. Finally the participant faced a mirror reflecting themselves, and s/he was asked, 'Are you ready to make a pledge to yourself to be your own parent and friend and take full responsibility for your life and yourself?' If the answer was a convincing *yes*, s/he claimed back the final stone and was ceremonially welcomed to adulthood.

EXERCISE

◆ Place your four stones in the order mother, father, sibling, peer, and behind them a mirror together with the fifth stone. Approach the first stone and demand return of any power you feel your mother still holds. When you feel you have really got it back, go on to the next and so on. When you get to the mirror, see yourself and ask yourself, 'am I ready to pledge myself to be my own parent and friend and to take full responsibility for my self and my life?'

◆ When you feel the answer is yes, pick up the fifth stone and retire with your journal and write down what this means for you and how it feels. Place the five stones on your personal altar or where they will act as constant reminders of your pledges to yourself.

The next part is re-parenting to our true parents, Mother Earth and Father Sun. The next day we set up an altar outside to Mother Earth to the west and to Father Sun to the east. Everybody participated in the creations, which were made out of nature from what was available without harming anything. Soon two beautiful altars were ready. We chanted and drummed together while each member went to the west altar to kneel and make prayers to the Earth as their true mother, and then to the east to shout to the sky and make prayers to the Sun as their true father. We completed with thanksgiving and an offering of tobacco. There was a palpable feeling of connectedness and good spirit.

EXERCISE

◆ Find a place in nature where you can perform a ceremony in this way. Make a simple but beautiful altar to the west on the earth for the Earth, and to the east for the Sun. Go to the Earth altar and kneel on the earth. Feel the Earth and acknowledge her as your true mother. It is she who gave birth to you, nurtures you, feeds you, breathes you. You are part of her.

◆ Then go to the east altar and call to the Sun and the sky. Acknowledge the Sun as your true father. The Sun is the fire within you, the provider of warmth and light, the Sun fires the plants to grow, the Sun bathes the earth in her rays, you exist as part of the Sun.

◆ When you feel complete make a small offering, give your altars back to nature, and, as a warrior, leave the place as if you had never been there.

Our ceremony had another whole part – a three-day-and-night vision quest in the mountains of Wales. A challenge suitable for an adult. (Vision quests are discussed in Chapter 7.)

There was also a final part when we engineered that the group take over from the three of us who had been leaders, so they became leaders and teachers themselves, while we became participants in the activities they arranged.

CHAPTER 5

Petty Tyrants

The irritating, annoying, difficult people of life and the many gifts they bring

I N THE COURSE of our lives many people and situations appear to test our mettle. A good name for these is petty tyrants. In Carlos Castaneda's famous works, his teacher don Juan explains to him the value of petty tyrants in his life to irritate, challenge and annoy the hell out of him and thus to teach him sobriety, patience, fortitude, forbearance, self-discipline and other such excellent qualities. At one point he suggests that a spiritual warrior who has no petty tyrants should go out and look for one!

All petty tyrants are, in effect, positive energy misused. They are motivated by fear and from that they feel the need to control. In other words they have little trust in the universe or themselves. The map of the medicine wheel based on the eight directions of the Twenty Count (see Chapter 7) and the Star Maiden's Circle provides a marvellous map of the manifestations of petty tyrant behaviour and how to respond creatively to it. We all have to deal with difficult people in our lives, it is a part of our journey and an art to be learned. Difficult people reflect difficult parts of ourselves. They are life's external reflections of work to be done on the internal. And, heaven forbid, it is just possible that from time to time we ourselves might be experienced as petty tyrants by others!

I have conducted a weekend workshop many times over the years which has had the prosaic title of 'The Way of the Warrior' and later the rather more to the point title of 'Fun and Games with the Tyrants of Life'. What I would like to do is take you through the essence of that workshop in such a way that you can gain a sense of understanding of the types of people who get under your skin. It will also introduce the strategies they use which may get to you and the strategies you can use to hold your own and even get the better of them.

First of all let us look at the medicine-wheel map. Nowhere else have I seen such a wonderful map of life's problem people.

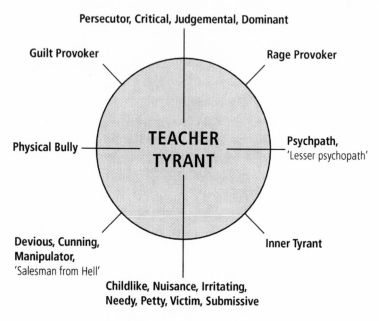

The medicine wheel of petty tyrants

The south tyrant

We start with the south direction. The south is the direction of the past and of the inner child and emotions. Its qualities are being able to see 'close to' and to challenge emotional fear and find a sense of trust and innocence in one's attitude to life. The tyrant is the needy, bothersome, nuisance, irritating sort of person who provokes you to become unreasonable, like a child on its worst behaviour, a great challenge to emotional stability. Around a childlike tyrant it is very difficult to keep your cool because their talent is to get the better of you and then take your power by making you feel guilty. Know anyone like that?

Here are some strategies to try. Firstly, you need to keep your emotional reactions firmly under wraps or else you lose right away. Secondly, you could interrupt their patterns and distract them, perhaps give them a task to do or in some way refocus them on something other than you. You could be consciously illogical and distracting yourself, ignoring their whingeing – or whatever is their ploy – and doing some yourself, going off at a tangent and so changing the focus of their consciousness and preventing them from pulling you into their story.

It is good to remember that all tyrants – as all people – basically seek love, attention, acceptance, support, care, understanding and all good things like that. It is just that some, out of deep wounding, have the most extraordinarily convoluted ways of attempting to get it.

The north tyrant

Opposite to the south is the north tyrant. This is the place of mind and thinking, of the everyday adult persona who organises life and plans for the future. It is the 'knowing' place, the place of knowledge, but the tyrant is the one who doesn't know and doesn't trust and dare not show any of that, so a big cover-up job is required. This becomes the tyrant face of the person which, to maintain ego and deny fear, becomes the blamer and persecutor and is judgmental, critical and mind-controlling.

Do you ever find you feel a little better because someone else is down? This is an expression of the little, separated ego-self. It gets expressed as the archetypal 'boss' of all bosses or the great one-upmanship champion. All bullies whether physical, or as in this case, mental, are sad and lonely souls crying for help, for someone to take notice of them, crying to be seen as someone of value. All of which means that the real issue is they do not value and esteem themselves.

Strategies start with watching your own reactions and checking what gets to you. When they put you down, do you believe it or some part of it? Check what that is about, what is it showing you about yourself? Then see if you can muster the skill to play tit for tat with them. Try to match their mind speed and stop them walking over you by having a powerful response at the ready. This is not easy but it feels just great when you do it for the first time and you watch them back off.

Another strategy is to praise them for their quickness of mind and insight and ask them to teach you. This is a bit creepy but it can take the wind out of their sails quite successfully.

Always be aware of the physical space. The critical tyrant often has trappings such as imposing clothes, office, big desk and so on, things to make you feel s/he is bigger than you. Remember this is only necessary because s/he doubts him/herself. No one has to be self-important unless they feel inadequate. They are little boys and little girls masquerading as adult, powerful people, struggling to make *themselves* feel okay.

The west tyrant

Situated in the west of the wheel is the place of the physical, the body, the earth, matter and the present moment. The tyrant of this direction is the physical bully who seeks to dominate, to control the space, to invade your territory, to play primitive, primate pecking-order politics. By imposing his will over others, he seeks to feed his self-esteem and become king of the castle.

The first essential strategy is to keep a wary eye on the physical space. The bully will try to keep you in an inferior place so attempt to move to an equal or higher place. Keep a good handle on your emotions and do not be phased by threats. Use humour to defuse the situation if you can. Bullies are just little people trying to be big because they do not feel good enough as they are.

The east tyrant

The place of fire, of spirit, of timelessness, of the magical aspect of the inner child is the east of the wheel. When we enter this part of our consciousness we go beyond little ego-self, beyond 'I' and into beingness, existence, and we are fully involved in whatever we are doing to the exclusion of self-consciousness. The tyrant of this direction is the opposite of this, it is spirit gone wrong, fire gone out of control, the magical child gone neurotic. The major tyrant is the psychopath, the character with dead eyes who is potentially highly dangerous because he has lost his soul and will think nothing of ridding you of yours. The recommended strategy if you happen to be unfortunate enough to meet one is to run like hell or else act insanely. You acting insanely is the one thing they are not equipped to deal with, it is not in their agenda for how you are supposed to react.

The east tyrant we are more likely to have to deal with is what I like to call the 'Lesser Psychopath'. These are fascinating, charismatic characters. The ability of us ordinary humans to follow these people and give our power, money, rights, decisions, etc. to a charismatic leader figure who knows 'the truth' and is 'nearer to God', never ceases to astonish me. Never more so than when I have done it myself (fortunately not often and not for long). These people circulate the story that they have access to powers you do not have, are beyond ordinariness, and have either a direct line to 'God', or some cosmic mission of superior importance. And the key word is importance. They catch ordinary mortals by appealing to self-importance and glamour. 'Stick with me, my disciples, and one day you could be up on the dais and you could have adoring followers just like me. You could be the great leader sitting under the lights and you could have lovely girls/boys at your feet ready and aching to do your every bidding, and it could be you being driven around in the Rolls Royce. It could be you!

Remember that every follower who adores the 'great leader' actually, desperately, wants to be there in his/her place. What is really loved is the limelight, the glory, the glamour, the importance. If the great leader shows special favour to a devotee, that person almost faints in the power of sheer self-important, self-adoring glory. Nowhere is this phenomenon more pervasive than in 'spiritual' organisations because the ultimate desire of most of us is to be nearer to God in some way. And so if 'ashram-think' has it that your guru is practically God, then all you have to do is give yourself to the guru (ladies and young boys first, of course) and you will be practically enlightened. Even if you are not, all your fellow disciples will treat you with awe and reverence, so what is the difference? You are special, so you must be more enlightened than the others.

The necessary strategy is to be aware of the effect that all the trappings, the promulgated belief system and the glamour have on you. Do you get drawn in and hooked and if so what part of you is responding? Is it the part of you that wants to serve the people and the planet or is it the part of you that wants glory and fame and importance? And most importantly, take a careful look at the transfer of power, at where the power is going. Watch how yours and others' egos are either given glamour, importance and perhaps even a special position or else thoroughly trampled and demolished. Remember, psychopaths feel really powerless and dreadful inside – more so than any other tyrant – otherwise they would not have to make themselves the centre of so much fuss.

The south-west tyrant

Now let us move to the non-cardinal points, the moving energies. Firstly the south-west. The south-west is the power of the 'dream', so the tyrant is the one who sucks on your dream for their own purposes. A good south-west tyrant discovers your ego-desires, your ambitions, your wish for glamour, your selfish little needs, and then plays a tune on them so you end up, for example, buying something beyond your means because it will add to your feeling of importance and worth – especially in the eyes of the tyrant who you now dearly want to impress. When he succeeds, you become like the emperor with no clothes. You look around and the tyrant is wearing your suit!

We have all met con people and I doubt if there is a single person who has not been conned and has conned others from time to time. It is part of human life, and animal life too, such as the cuckoo who lays her eggs in another bird's nest and whose offspring ultimately throw out all the foster parent's own children.

The strategies for dealing with this tyrant start with the need for emotional discipline while watching your ego being praised or undermined. Also watch the use of physical space because this tyrant too will subtly try to put you at a disadvantage. A firm 'no' or a very conditional 'yes', and whatever you do *never sign anything* when in their presence. Do not be above the need to be cunning and devious yourself in these situations. Stay humble and above all remember, *caveat emptor* – let the buyer beware. That means you.

I happened to see a fascinating television programme recently about 'salesmen from hell' which, with the aid of hidden cameras, demonstrated the skilled use of seriously devious, cunning, manipulative tactics to get people to buy very expensive goods whether they could afford them or not, or even needed them. It reminded me that some years ago I had someone come to my home to demonstrate an adjustable bed. The bed was excellent with two ways of electrically adjusting the mattress and two gentle vibrators which gently shook the whole thing and gave a relaxing massage. I was severely tempted to buy except for the price of around £4,000. (Credit available no problem, only so much a week, you can have it all *now*.) Later I found similar beds in a furniture shop starting at about £600, so was thankful that my natural hesitation and doubt had saved me a lot of cash.

The north-east tyrant

Now let us go across the wheel and look at the north-east tyrant. The north-east of the wheel is the place of choice, of the design and choreography of energy, of our free will to make decisions. The skill of this tyrant is to take this ability away from you and use it themselves to gain advantage over you. They make you so infuriated that you cannot think straight, and then enjoy the way you are at their mercy. You lose yourself, your cool and your clarity while the tyrant plays innocent. This is the skill of the rage provoker who gets people furious yet one cannot somehow pin it on them. They push your buttons yet it is very difficult to find an adequate response that does not leave you feeling an idiot. Anyone ever do that to you? You bet the tyrant has sussed your fears, your weaknesses and your self-importance traps.

So let's have some strategies. Firstly, it is necessary to draw your boundaries very clearly. Secondly, self-control is not easy with a really good rage provoker so it may serve you best to leave and cool down. The more you defend yourself, the more power they have to disempower you. Some of these tyrants are energy vampires and you can find yourself used up and wilting in their presence. Take a deep breath, centre yourself, and remember it is all a game.

The place of the rage provoker is opposite to the south-west which is all about your dreams, wishes and hopes. Look to your own south-west for the hook the tyrant has in you. What is he appealing to or demolishing of your dreams and hopes? What might you want from him and hope to get? Do you secretly want to impress this person? Take a clear look and see if you can come to a place of wanting nothing, then you can deal with such a tyrant much more easily.

The north-west tyrant

Now we come to my favourite tyrant of all, in the north-west direction. This is the guilt provoker. This tyrant uses responsibility, rules, blame and shame to get his/her way over you. You are their 'mark' and they have an organised plan as to how you are going to feel and what you are going to be pushed to do for them.

By the way – have you phoned your mother (or father) today? You haven't? You haven't phoned your poor old dear mother who worked her fingers to the bone for you, bringing you up from the days when you were just a helpless little baby? Who suffered so you could come into the world? You haven't shown that you care, you haven't been concerned for your only mother who might have been injured or even died while you just sit here reading a book? Your mother thinks of you and worries about you all the time and what do you do for her? Nothing. Yes, alright so you sent her a Mother's Day card last year, but I'm talking about now, what are you doing for her now?

I love to do a tirade like that when teaching a workshop. It is amazing how many people relate to it. It seems to be a sort of universal guilt theme of our culture. The most important thing to remember with guilt is that it only works if the recipient believes it.

Remember your guilt provoker needs you. Without you, yes *you*, they cannot get what they want – your attention, 'love', dependence, attachment, support, gossipy agreement about the shortcomings of others to bolster their ego and co-dependence. You are the key to their happiness, survival, existence even. You are responsible – without *you* they will suffer, and just whose fault do you think that will be?

Now for strategies. Watch your beliefs and any tendency you have towards feeling guilty. The guilt provoker's whole ploy depends on you believing their story and believing you are responsible for them. If you do not buy their story, you do not get caught in the trap. Be aware of what is really going on. As with everything else, it is *awareness* that sets us free.

Other helpful strategies. Take guilt provokers literally and respond to just what they say, not what they imply. Use humour, laugh at their strictures, deflate them. Distract them, interrupt their pattern, move around, make a cup of tea at the wrong time, sit in the 'wrong' chair, change the subject, tell a joke. They may get very angry at you but you will have to put up with that and stand firm. This is your challenge to be strong and hold your power. The benefit is feeling good about yourself. The penalty for giving in is knowing you have been beaten and feel weak and feeble later on when it sinks in that you have lost.

The inner tyrant

Now we come to the last and most important tyrant of all, the one who really matters and who holds the key to the whole problem of people who get to you and push your buttons. Yes folks, it's *you*. It's your *inner tyrant* – the ultimate tyrant is our very own self. How we feel about ourself deep inside, both consciously, sub-consciously and unconsciously in our deepest recesses, determines how much we are at the mercy of outside tyrants and how much we draw them to us by sending out subliminal signals.

The tyrants who appear in your life repeatedly are the ones that you draw towards you for necessary lessons. They hold the energies you have most internalised. They point you to the inner work you need to do the most. Each tyrant is a gift from the universe to help you clean up your life-act.

Opposites

The medicine wheel teaches us a lot when we look at the powers of the opposite direction. When seeking to gain back your power and put a tyrant in his place, look to the opposite place on the wheel. We have covered some of this but here are some more insights.

For example on the north-east–south-west axis, the rage provoker attempts to take over your ability to make your own choices and so you need to look at your 'dream' (south-west) and make sure you are not deflected from your life purpose. Remember who you are and why you are here and be aware of which of your wishes and hopes they are using to get at you. You have to be very self-honest about your own ego desires and self-importance because this is their strongest ally and your strongest enemy.

In the opposite corner the devious manipulator endeavours to redirect your 'dream', and so by placing your awareness opposite in the choices you are about to make and keeping them firmly in line with your life aims, you can avoid getting pulled into an ego-trap and having your energy and money taken from you. Again it is your self-importance that is your weakness. Without self-importance we are very strong against all tyrants.

On the west-east line, the physical bully hits you to dis-spirit you so that you give up and give in. Whether you win or lose the short-term physical battle, it is more important that you keep in touch with your spirit and win the long-term struggle.

The pyschopath has lost his spirit and sees you therefore as being without spirit and so has no compunction about relieving you of your body if it suits him/her. Hence he/she is highly dangerous and it is best to get far away if you can. The lesser psychopath sees you as food for his/her grandiosity and power, another slave for the empire of his/her self-importance. Look at your own self-importance traps and feel the earth beneath your feet. Stay grounded.

On the south–north axis, the childlike, needy tyrant attempts to control your emotions. Look to the north of the wheel and use your mind skills to stay aware of the game and use your mental control to check your emotions and play whatever counter-game is most effective and helpful.

The persecutor, judgmental, tyrant criticises you – for your own good, of course – and attempts to press every worthlessness button you have until you get lost in emotionality and are jelly at his mercy. Look opposite to the south and use emotional discipline and remember your own worth regardless of this onslaught.

Lastly on the north-west–south-east axis, we have already spoken about the guilt provoker and how s/he can do nothing unless you buy the story and take on the guilt. Opposite in the south-east corner is the inner tyrant and all your history, and that is where the work is: to 'erase your personal history', to heal the wounds of your life so they no longer have any effect on you. This is where any guilt and shame are held and where we all have work to do to heal ourselves and keep moving towards freedom.

Finally give thanks to life for the challenges of all the tyrants who come your way. Without them life might be just plain sailing and then what would you learn? I mean – imagine James Bond without a worthy villain, Harry Potter without Lord Voldemort, Bill Clinton without a libido, or Frasier without a giant ego. What fun would the world be then?

All competent tyrants move around the wheel

When you study them you find that most tyrants use two or three positions to get you off balance and to get their way over you. For example, the poor-me, whingeing, south tyrant who, when s/he has got you into the place of giving up – 'Alright, for God's sake just tell me what you really want!' – will turn on a knife edge and become a dominant, persecuting north tyrant, and perhaps also a wickedly competent north-west guilt provoker, telling you all that is wrong with you. Or the south-west manipulator failing to get his way with you who promptly uses his skill to suss your weak points, pushing all your buttons like crazy, and combining that with a good dose of the critical and judgmental with a little guilt thrown in for good measure. Does that describe anyone you know?

In the end it is our self-knowledge, self-acceptance, self-understanding and self-love that will save us from the grip of the tyrant. When we feel good inside, know and accept that we are not perfect but are worthy, know that all tyrants at some level are unhappy, insecure, people who are suffering inside and that the person who most suffers from their behaviour is themself, then we can keep our shields in their rightful places – keep our emotions disciplined, our mind awake and aware, our body at the ready and our sense of humility and humour intact. Then we can disable the tyrant and perhaps create understanding and compassion out of the chaos.

The Native Americans have an expression – 'counting coup'. It means getting the better of an opposer by showing them their weaknesses. From this place change can take place for the better.

The ultimate aim of 'counting coup' is to turn enemy into friend. When someone who has been a tyrant shows you respect, you know you have mastered some aspect of yourself. By healing and making friends with a separated part of your self, you can now make friends with the person who reflected that for you.

Teacher tyrant

The most competent tyrant of all is the teacher tyrant who is able to put on any tyrant 'mask' with consciousness and without ego in order to teach, test and help the student develop. Castaneda's don Juan was such a teacher, and at times he frightened Carlos out of his wits in order to shift his perception – which it seems he did most successfully.

A good teacher keeps the student aware and awake. While on the one hand creating a feeling of great safety and security so that the student can let down all defences and be real, on the other hand keeping the student on his toes, discerning and aware that, in life, the only person one can ultimately trust is oneself, and even that takes work. Deep trust in oneself takes a lot of discipline over the automatic self-indulgent robot-self. To be able to trust oneself totally means to have to overcome one's addictions, attachments, dependencies, self-pity, comparisons, expectations, needs for approval – the Seven Shadow Arrows (see Chapter 3). That is a lifetime's work in itself for most of us.

It is good to remember that all tyrants are teachers sent by life. They are only a problem to the extent that we have work to do on ourselves. When we feel good and are in harmony, alignment and balance, they are merely a tickle. It is when we are out of balance that they get to us, spin our shields and leave us feeling insecure, deflated and perhaps even terrible. They show us our weaknesses and petty desires, and where the work is required. A tyrant vanquished – once we have changed inside – becomes a friend.

EXERCISE

◆ Select an irritating and annoying person in your life and consciously appoint them to be your teacher. (Whatever you do, don't tell them.) Your task is to change your attitude from resentment, bitterness, anger – or whatever it may be – to one of conscious acceptance that life has sent you this person to teach you something – perhaps many things.

♦ Study the person and their devices. How do they get to you? What are the weaknesses that they find in you? How do they get under your skin? Where do they make you feel hurt, and therefore what egocentric self-importance do they provoke?

♦ Identify their techniques and put them on the wheel. In which direction do you need to stand in order to do combat? Use the strategies described above as a basis for an overall plan together with the strategies appropriate to the directions the petty tyrant is coming from. Remember you are working to change your own patterns so that the petty tyrant can no longer get one over you. When you change, they have to. You can only change yourself, no one else, the work is within you. You will get feedback as soon as you succeed because the situation will change.

Many years ago when I first came to London I shared a house with several friends amongst whom was a woman who soon began to manifest some of my mother's worst traits. Little did I know but my instinctive fear responses were similar to traits in her father that she detested. So we had a sort of love–hate relationship which would periodically erupt in a volley of shouting. She was a most effective critical, judgmental, persecuting tyrant to me and it was only when I did something about the wimpish fear-riddled side of me that things changed and we became proper friends, which we still are nearly 20 years later. It was hard at the time but in retrospect it was a most valuable life lesson and I bless her for it.

Whatever tyrants are on your case, take it as an opportunity to challenge your old patterns, develop yourself and become stronger. That is what you are here for, to develop yourself into the best you can be. It is nothing to do with what anyone else is doing, your journey is yours alone, your talents and gifts uniquely yours alone and your burdens and blind spots are yours alone too. You are the only hero/heroine on your journey and your demons and dragons are there for you, and no one else, to do battle with.

WALKING THE BLUE ROAD

CHAPTER 6

Shamanic journeys

Experiencing multi-dimensional realities

THE BLUE ROAD is the road from west of the wheel to east. It is the road of moving through the now and the physical of the west to the timeless and transcendence of the east. To walk the Blue Road we are going to learn the traditional shamanic journey. This has been practised all over the world by our ancestors and is one of the most universal shamanic practices.

The shaman journeys to meet with spirits who may be regarded as power animals, spirit guides, ancestors, deceased shamans, even as gods, goddesses or angels, and who are seen as beings with great wisdom and power who are willing to help and guide the living. For us Westerners embarking on this way, we are likely to be touching into journeys of modest depth and it is likely to be some time before we become an out-of-body cosmic traveller who, in the words of Mercia Eliade 'commands the techniques of ecstacy – that is, because his soul can safely abandon his body and roam for vast distances, can penetrate the underworld and rise to the sky. Through his own ecstatic experience he knows the roads of the extraterrestrial regions.'

We start with learning to journey to non-ordinary reality and gain experience of these worlds. Now, whether these are 'real' worlds or 'only imagination' is a very interesting question which we need to address. From a scientific materialist point of view, it is just imagination and is all created by oneself and happens inside one's head. From a shamanic point of view, we travel to parallel but non-material worlds where spirits reside, and it all happens there. Apparently two

111

very different descriptions of experience. But let us look a little deeper at this thing called reality.

What comes first – reality or imagination? Was your house built before anyone thought of it? No, of course not. Someone thought of it, planned it, worked it all out, created it carefully in the imagination, and only finally the builders came and created 'reality': a physical house. Imagination definitely came first. You make a decision to do something – do you do the action or make the decision in your mind first? Of course you make the decision in your mind, in your imagination first and only then take the action. Where does your experience of life happen? Does it happen out there? No, of course not, it happens inside your consciousness. Life, when you think about it, is an internal experience, it all happens inside us. The outside world is the stimulus for reality which is our inner experience.

This question goes right back to how we see, frame, conceive, structure, our experience of Life, the Universe and Everything. We come to the question, 'what did the Creator create the universe out of?' Many a religionist will say, 'the ether', or something that was there. But if there was something there, another more primary Creator must have been around to create that first. The Ultimate Creator creates everything and by definition that must be so because the Creator is All-Mighty, but out of what? The only possible answer is out of self. Now we come to the point. The Creator creates creation out of all that there is, which is itself. Creation creates itself – the Creator imagines itself into the creation. The creation, as you will have noticed, is not a willy-nilly accident that just somehow works and makes sense. All the incredible balances of forces that keep galaxies and solar systems in balance are not just some accident, they are designed to do so with incredible subtlety that our science is nowhere near understanding yet. The Great Mystery of existence is a very vast Great Mystery of unimaginable ability and knowledge which expresses itself as the creation. Each of us is a cell in its body.

Are you an object to which things happen, or a part of the Creator – a co-creator with the Great Creator – of your experience of life? Where do you experience pain and pleasure, happiness and sadness? All your actual experience happens inside you. In that sense *all* your experience is in your imagination. So now the question, 'Is my inner experience a figment of my imagination or a world of spirit in its own right?' takes on a whole new perspective. There is no real difference. The more important question is, 'What am I experiencing in my inner self and how can I make it useful to me?' At workshops I like to assure the participants that the answer to the question – 'Is what I am experiencing real or imaginary?' – is a definitive *yes*.

The drum – the 'shaman' horse

Journeying is a method of entering an altered state of consciousness and is similar to meditation and hypnosis and all such ways of relaxing the body and withdrawing the consciousness from the everyday. There is one difference, however. The shamanic state of consciousness is purposeful, there is always a reason for going there. You need an intent, a clear purpose for seeking assistance from the spirits of other worlds. Traditionally it is facilitated with the 'shaman's horse' – the drum – beat at a steady 200–220 beats a minute, approximately equivalent to theta brainwaves. This helps to still mind-chatter and helps you to focus while you journey. Many people who have previously been accustomed to guided visualisation find a great revelation on their first experience of journeying with the drum – it feels so much more real.

The usual way the drum is played is with a steady beat. At the end of the journey, the call-back will sound, usually four or five slow beats repeated four times. Then the drum is beaten very quickly and you make your way back the way you went but more quickly.

In Chapter 1 we discussed the concept of the Lower, Middle and Upperworlds of parallel reality, now let us look more closely at the lower world.

The Lowerworld is the world of instinctual knowing and relates to the part of ourselves below the heart, our solar plexus with its fibres connecting with the world, our *hara* or *dantien*, the seat of personal power, and our base *chakra* with its primal energy, sexuality and creativity. When our instincts are fully functioning and in tune with life around us, we live with a deep sense of knowing and connection.

When out of tune, we are living with a great loss of power and ability to know and stand up for our truth. Interestingly, in the past this world was demonised and made into Hell and Hades and something to be feared, while the Upperworld was eulogised and made into the realm of God and light. But the Lowerworld is the world of Mother Earth and we are here in earth-made body-temples in order to learn how to live in this realm and to benefit from its many lessons. Like dark and light, the Lower and Upperworlds are pairs, one of which cannot function without the other.

Most of the helpful spirits of the Lowerworld are easily perceived as animals, occasionally as humans or mythical beings. Generally speaking, the Lowerworld appears just like a natural landscape in this world, and, when journeying, everything one experiences is of relevance and has a symbolic or even a literal meaning.

It is important to point out there are no such 'things' as power animals. These are spirit-energies that we most often perceive as animals because they are the picture and sense-forms in which we can most easily comprehend the spirit energies and receive their messages.

Trial journey to the Lowerworld

To make this journey you will need a quiet place and either a friend with a drum or a shamanic drumming CD or tape and personal stereo with earphones.

There is a traditional posture for journeying to the Lowerworld which comes from South America. This is the one Michael Harner teaches in his workshops, and he describes in his book *The Way of the Shaman* (Bantam, 1980) being taught it by the Jivaro Indians of Ecuador. It is very simple, you lie on your back and cover your eyes with your left arm or the back of your hand.

EXERCISE

◆ Smudge yourself by bathing yourself in the smoke from burning sage or light an incense stick to help get into a feeling of 'sacred space', lie down comfortably and adopt the posture described above. It is good to either cover your eyes with a cloth or darken the room. Switch on the CD or tape.

◆ For the first journey let us just visit and observe. Speak your objective out loud, 'I am journeying to the Lowerworld to visit and observe'.

◆ Let your breathing slow down as you consciously relax your muscles and feel the gravity of Mother Earth holding you. Then visualise a place which you actually know from which you can easily imagine travelling down into the earth. It might be a hollow tree, a disused mine shaft or well, the bottom of a lake or ocean, perhaps something as ordinary as an underground railway station. Let yourself 'be there' and as the drumming starts, enter the tunnel which will take you into the earth. Firstly you may meet the 'guardian of the Lowerworld' and if it is a good day to travel, the guardian will let you through (if not, return and try another day). The tunnel will slope down and will probably become steeper as you go. Let it carry you down, down, down, deeper and deeper into the earth. If you come across an obstruction, just go round it or find a gap through. Continue down until you find yourself deep down under the earth in a cave. Look for a path which will lead you outside. Follow the path out into a natural landscape. Look around you and examine what is there. Nearby is your own personal power place. Go there and look around. Be aware if it is day or night, sunny or rainy, still or windy, if you are in forest, open meadow, barren wasteland or gentle woodland. Are you near running water, is the land fertile or desert, can you hear birdsong and are there animals around? While exploring the landscape, keep track of where you are, and when the call-back comes, return to the cave or entrance to the tunnel and come back up to the ordinary world.

Once you have journeyed enough to feel happy with the method, it is a good idea to go searching for your power animal. I say animal, but you may have more than one. There is no limit to the number nor to how they appear to you. Remember they are energy which you are perceiving in the form of an animal or maybe a bird. Sometimes they may take reptile form and very occasionally even an insect such as a spider.

Power animal retrieval journey

This journey is similar to the previous one, but here we communicate with our power animal. Remember that in the dreamworld, we communicate with dream language, rarely linear words which are an invention of the third dimension.

EXERCISE

◆ Take the same journey described above but this time state your intention clearly to meet and retrieve your power animal(s). When you get to your personal power place, call your animal(s) to come to you and wait and see what happens. When an animal comes, to be sure it is your animal, look in the four directions, one after the other. If the animal shows up all four times, you can be pretty sure it is for you. If you are uncertain, ask the animal straight. It will give you a truthful answer or indicate by body language.

◆ When you have made contact with your animal, call the animal to you and, when the drum sounds the return, carry it back in your arms to this world where it is energy.

Retrieving a power animal is like plugging back into a power source. At times in our life when we get dispirited and down, we have, from a shamanic point of view, lost power. These are the times when we can be subject to accidents or what appears to be 'bad luck'; although there is no such thing as bad luck or good luck. These are indications that all is not well and we are power-less; it is time to take a journey to reconnect and restore power.

In the old cultures the shaman would do the journeying while the apprentice or helper drummed. In today's world it feels appropriate for each of us to learn to journey for ourselves and restore our own power, and in workshops that is what we teach first. However, once one is familiar with one's own Lower and Upperworlds, it is very revealing and informative to journey for someone else. Soul retrieval is much easier when done for someone else and more effective because it is a giving from one to another.

There are many books with classifications of meanings of power animals such as the excellent *Medicine Cards* by Jamie Sams. However, when you journey it is *your* psyche that throws up the image, and so the first question to be pondered is, 'What does it represent to me?' When journeying in the Lowerworld there is one great source of information: the animal itself. When in doubt ask your animal.

Journeying for help and guidance with life

A good journey to do next after retrieving your power animal and becoming familiar with him/her can be a journey to ask a major life question. Just one question per journey, and it is important to get it really clear. Power animals, in my experience, will not bother much with messy unthought-out questions and are likely to express disgust unless one goes to them having done one's own share of the work.

EXERCISE

Sit down quietly and consider what is most important in your life right now. On what aspect of your life would it serve you most to have increased clarity right now? What do you feel you most need help with at this moment? It may be a very practical question.

For example, here is a Howard Charing story. (Howard is my partner in Eagle's Wing Centre for Contemporary Shamanism.) Howard wanted to sell his MGB, a classic(ish) car and he advertised it and did all the usual necessary things. No matter what, it just would not sell, no one was interested. Finally it occurred to him to use his own medicine on the problem, so he took a journey to ask the spirits. The message he received was to get the car into first-class condition with everything working and then it would bring a buyer to it. He took it to the garage and got it fixed and in beautiful order. As he was parking it on return from the garage, a neighbour who had shown interest but rejected the car previously, strolled up to him and asked if it was still for sale. The car was promptly sold.

The Lowerworld spirits can assist us with very practical, nitty-gritty details of life. It is always good to remember that everything is spiritual just as everything is secular. The spirit is everywhere and in everything so what is the difference? So if you have what might seem too mundane and practical a question to ask spirit, do not let any such idea put you off. Most of life is a series of mundane happenings which add up to a magical existence in a body-spacesuit on planet Earth. But it is all the little details which add up to the whole.

EXERCISE CONTINUED

So write down your question and hone it till it feels right. Best if it is a what or how question rather than a yes or no. Then set yourself up as before and take a journey. Go down the tunnel as before but notice any changes. Your power animal may meet you in the tunnel or even at the entrance, and if so be ready to follow him if he indicates to you. Otherwise simply get down to the cave and go to your power place and call your animal to come to you, and present your question and see what happens. Remember if your animal turns away, it most probably means, 'follow me'.

Journey to the four directions

A very good journey to do for reflection on your life is a journey to all four directions. Your intent can be phrased like this: 'I journey to the four directions for guidance, help and reflection on my life right now.'

EXERCISE

- Set up your space and yourself as before and journey down to meet your power animal. Ask your power animal to guide you to the four directions, starting with the south.

- Travel south to the place of water, emotion, the past, the inner child, your personal history, the 'close-to' place where you may wrestle between fear of being and expressing your full self and the joy of living with trust and innocence knowing you are an honoured part of the universe. Simply, with awareness, see what is shown to you. Stay as long as feels right and note what is reflected of you and your life at this time.

- Then move on to the west, the place of earth and mineral, of the physical and the body, of the 'dream' that is our life, the 'looks-within' place where the joy of daring to live life fully and vibrantly and the struggle against inertia and deadness takes place. Watch and see what is shown to you, what messages, indication and guidance you receive.

- When this feels complete, turn to the north and go in that direction. The north is the place of the four winds, air, the mind, thought, the way we structure our experience of life, our plans and hopes for the future. It is the 'knowing place' where we wrestle between knowledge and bullshit, between daring to live by what our 'knowing' tells us as against what the consensus would have us believe. See and listen to what you are shown and told in the north.

- Then lastly go east. The east is the place of fire, of the magical child inside us and the timeless realm we touch when we let go and enter the place of total involvement where there is no 'I' to limit us. It is the place of choice, if we let it be so, and the place of illumination and power. East is where we can soar above and 'see far', the whole picture, the wider perspective. Spend whatever time you need in the east and let the impressions come to you.

- Then it is time to thank your power animal and any other spirits who have assisted you. Be ready for any last messages they may give you.

Then make your way back to the cave and up the tunnel and return to ordinary reality.

◆ Make notes of your journey. It is good to look again at what you have written after about two weeks as you may see more in it than is obvious to you now.

Journeys to illuminate ancestral gifts and burdens

We have looked at personal history in our travels on the Red Road, but it is good to do so using tools of the Blue Road as well. We can journey and see what the spirits have to teach us and show us about what we have inherited from our ancestors. Our personal history issues go back many generations as ways of being are passed down, on and on. It is only when someone steps determinedly on to the road of personal development and self-mastery that a significant change of a lineage takes place. Otherwise the same old stuff tends to go on and on being dumped by each generation on to the next. We must remember that it is not just burdens of our ancestors that are passed on, it is also their gifts, talents and abilities. These are just as important, as they are the blessings we have each received and are the best part of our inheritance.

First, however, let us journey to see what are the burdens we carry from our ancestral line. This can shed considerable light upon habits, proclivities, dead areas, addictions, self-sabotage and so on, and point to what has been given us to heal. In doing so we also heal our line.

EXERCISE

◆ Prepare yourself as before, state your intent clearly: 'I journey to the Lowerworld to meet my power animal and to ask for understanding of the burdens I carry from my ancestors.'

- Then enter into the journey. Go down the tunnel and meet your power animal. Speak your intent again and see what happens.

- On return write your experience in your journal.

Now journey for the other side of the coin:

EXERCISE

- 'I journey to the Lowerworld to meet my power animal and to ask for understanding of the gifts, talents and abilities that are given to me from my ancestral line.'

- Again write down your experience.

Look at both journeys. What does the one say about the other?

Journeys with a partner

It is one thing travelling to your own other worlds, but greater revelation awaits when you travel to someone else's. In fact it is often easier to experience another's world than your own because you tend to go with a lot less wishful thinking and many fewer conditions. It can be a revelation to find out just how connected we are and how little separation there really is between us.

For these next exercises you need a friend who is willing and, hopefully, enthusiastic to partner you. A good way to begin is for each of you to take an exploratory journey to the other's Lowerworld. One of you journeys while the other simply takes a rest. It is optional as to whether you narrate the journey as you go – I find this very helpful as it keeps me focussed and somehow 'solidifies' the journey as it happens – or you may prefer to stay silent and convey your experience at the end.

Lie down side by side just touching. A good way is toe to toe, knee to knee, hip to hip and shoulder to shoulder. It is not all necessary but it is a good way to start as it will keep reminding you that you are journeying for your friend instead of yourself.

EXERCISE

♦ State your intention clearly: 'I am journeying to meet my power animal and visit and explore the Lowerworld of [name your partner].'

♦ Journey down the tunnel as usual and meet your power animal. You may very well find a side opening that was not there before. This is likely to lead directly to your friend's lower world, so travel down and see where you come out. Call your power animal to join you and explore the landscape, remember everything has a meaning. Do not worry if you are surprised, just accept it as it is shown to you. If your power animal turns away, he is probably leading you to show you something, so just follow. If you are narrating, just narrate what you see and sense. You are in the same world as the dreamworld and communications occur as energy which we experience as images, senses and feelings, and which we usually have to translate in order to make sense.

Caveat regarding journeying for another

This is something that happens extremely rarely, but nevertheless once in a blue moon you might see something difficult. A possible death, child abuse, a warning of an accident, something of that nature, where direct communication might be traumatic. In such a case, hold back and share what you can later, rather than directly as you are journeying. Sensitivity at all times.

Hide and seek

This is a partner journey which is really fun and is also good training:

EXERCISE

The idea is that one of you journeys down the tunnel into the Lowerworld and hides. About 30–40 seconds later the other one follows and tries to find you. When you hide it is necessary to be very clear where you are and to stay there. For example you go down and find a lake with a circle of trees at one end. If you hide in the trees, it is very clear where you are. It is no good making it too difficult or being at all unclear where you see yourself as being – the clearer, the better. Your partner then follows you down with absolutely no idea of what you are seeing but with clear intent. 'I journey to the Lowerworld to find Mary.' The task is to sense where you are and what sort of place you are in. Afterwards compare notes and see what results you have. Then do it with the other partner following. This is a great journey to practise and develop your skills. Remember it is the feeling rather than the details that is most important.

Journey to receive a symbol for a partner

In this journey to the Lowerworld you ask for a symbol to present to your partner. Remember that the language of the parallel world is the language of symbols, the language of night dreams, so you are asking for guidance and help in the language of the place you are journeying to.

EXERCISE

♦ Again, prepare yourselves and lie down side by side as before. State your intention clearly: 'I journey to the Lowerworld to find and retrieve a symbol for my partner Mary.'

♦ Go to your place and enter the tunnel and travel down just as before. Like before you may be invited down a side tunnel direct to your partner's Lowerworld. If so, take it, if not go down to your world and ask your power animal to take you where you wish to go. When you get there ask to be shown a symbol which is relevant to your partner right now. Once you have it, return and then draw it for your partner.

♦ Discuss what meanings are shown by the symbol.

Journeys to the Upperworld

The Upperworld relates to the part of us above the heart: the throat centre of communication, the third eye of spirit sight, and the lotus at the top of the head which connects us to the cosmos. It is the home of more philosophical spirit guides, cosmic beings and great wise elders who appear to us usually in human form and whose wisdom is universal rather than specific. They guide us more towards seeing the overall lessons of an incarnation rather than what to do about a present problem. In some cultures an expectant mother will journey with the shaman to the land of the unborn to seek the purpose for which the child is being born. The child is then named to reflect the purpose of its birth.

The light in the Upperworld tends to be translucent and pastel coloured and the feeling is often ethereal. One very important point: the Upperworld is not in any way superior to the Lowerworld, just as on the medicine wheel, the east is not superior to the west. They are complimentary and equal and one could not exist without the other.

There are many ways of journeying to the Upperworld and some of them will probably be quite familiar. For example you may be familiar with Psychosynthesis, a form of psychotherapy that uses visualisation techniques to journey up a mountain to visit a 'Wise Person' who lives at the top. Other typical journeys are made by climbing a magic tree which goes miles up into the sky; by being lifted up by whirlwind or tornado; by climbing the Axis Mundi, the world tree. Many fairy tales and legends speak of this, such as 'Jack and the Beanstalk', although the giant Jack encounters is more of a typical Lowerworld image. As with the Lowerworld, the shaman can journey to the Upperworld to find help and guidance, though not usually to retrieve a power animal.

The Western 'dream', however, has got in here and mucked up the ancient symbology. In most Western traditions, the concepts of good and evil have become confused with upper and lower, and with light and dark. For example, in the Judaeo–Christian tradition, they have become Heaven and Hell, and in the Greek tradition, Mount Olympus where the good gods reside and Hades where the baddies are.

This is a split which desperately needs healing and re-mythologising in our collective Western psyche. While all the 'good' gods are in the sky realm of light and all the 'bad' ones down in the dark realm of earth in Hell or Hades, what hope is there for religious believers to value and love the Earth? Hell originally meant light and comes from the Greek *Helles*. Helen is the goddess of light. Also the Native American mythological Wyola-Helle, Goddess of the prairie, is known as Prairie-Light.

In Siberian shamanic mythology, the Creator gods live in the Upperworld but show little interest in the affairs of humans, while the gods who created Earth live in the Lowerworld and show great interest and concern for the affairs of people and can be called on for help by shamans. A very much more earth-friendly mythology.

Exploratory journey to the Upperworld

You can make this journey with the same drumbeat as for the Lowerworld or with relaxing music – New Age style or perhaps some classical pieces which are very mellow might work for you; Tibetan Bowls, or anything that gives you the feeling of relaxation, quiet and ease, and helps you to go into the place between the worlds.

EXERCISE

◆ Prepare yourself as before and make yourself comfortable. You may prefer to lie down or to sit, perhaps in a familiar meditation pose. There is no specific posture recommended for Upperworld journeying. Whatever works for you is best.

◆ State your intention clearly: 'I journey to the Upperworld to meet my wise guide and listen to his/her wisdom.'

◆ Go to your place of beginning just as for the Lowerworld journeys but ask to be shown a way upward. You may be shown a tree or perhaps a mountain to climb or a ladder may appear. Whatever appears, follow and proceed upwards, feeling your lightness. At some point you are likely to come to a place where there is a sort of membrane, something perhaps almost like a sticky cloud that gives a sense of division, which you need to pass through. This is an important separation between the ordinary world and the Upperworld and it marks the place where the two meet. Proceed through, exerting force if necessary. Once above this membrane look around you and see and feel where you now are. Notice who and what is there.

◆ The Upperworld feels different to the Lowerworld and is likely to be more ethereal, less 'real', not at all dense. It may be very colourful and 'fabulous'. You will find communication is like telepathy and images and feelings come directly into you.

◆ Explore and see what you find, what you experience. Return at the end the way you came.

Journey to the Upperworld to meet a wise guide

First of all formulate the question or issue on which you require help. Whilst the Lowerworld is appropriate for basic nitty-gritty life issues, the Upperworld is for longer term, more philosophical issues that require seeing from above. That, after all, is where the Upperworld is – above.

EXERCISE

Proceed just as before but this time stating your intention: 'I journey to the Upperworld to meet my wise elder and seek guidance and help on (state issue).' Journey upwards in your particular way, through the membrane, and on up into the sky realm or wherever it seems you are. Keep going up until you come to a place which feels like the home of your guide. Ask your guide to show him/herself to you. If it doesn't happen, go on up further until it does. When you are there, join your guide and pose your question and feel what transpires.

At the end, return the way you came and write your experience in your journal. It is always good to do this right away because you catch it before you forget it. Like dreams these images can go out of the mind if not caught quickly.

Soul retrieval

The process called soul retrieval is very ancient and is a way in which the shaman enters the inner world of the client/patient and assists in unfolding his/her life from within. By journeying into another's inner spirit world, one can affect the realm of cause. One can travel back in time, because in all worlds except this one there is no time, and one can change the cause of a past trauma that is still held in a person's energy body today.

To someone who has no knowledge or experience of exploration into other worlds and has accepted the bullshit of the 'consensus tabloid' reality, this might sound fantastic, but in the world of shamanism, it is an everyday tried-and-tested healing method. And I mean tried and tested – through actual practical experience for thousands of years.

Almost everybody has experienced soul loss. It certainly happened to me with traumas such as being sent away to boarding school at the age of eight, which I experienced as gross abandonment. What made it so difficult was that it was done 'because we love you'. If that's love, give me less of it was my feeling at the time.

I also experienced it around puberty when, partially due to my mother's menopausal problems, the family structure, such as it was, disintegrated for a time. At the same time I was at a public boarding school I detested. I remember how I went into 'survival mode' just to get through, squashed a large chunk of my life-force and did my best to feel, both emotionally and physically, as little as possible.

For those who suffered in this way there is help. There is an excellent course offered in London called *Boarding School Survivors* (see Resources), and Nick Duffell, who created the course, has written a somewhat harrowing book which I would like to recommend to all parents contemplating sending their children away to board. It is called *The Making of Them.*

Such problems as inability to get your life to work; difficulty in focussing and concentrating; a feeling of lack of connection to your emotional body; of being spaced-out and not really present; feeling as if you are an observer in the drama of your life rather than a full participant; an all-pervasive feeling of fear; severe depression; are all symptoms of soul loss. Chronic illness, especially repetitive bad health, can indicate soul loss and I think that some recent illnesses such as ME (myalgic encephalomyelitis) are often due to this.

The World Health Organisation has stated that depression is likely to be the second biggest cause of illness and death of humans in the future. A shamanic way of saying it is that soul loss is soon to be the second biggest cause. Either way it is a horrendous statistic and speaks volumes about the chronic failure of the Western dream.

In the shamanic world view, the ability to maintain good health is a matter of power. If the body is power-full – meaning power over one's self, of course, not manipulative power over others, and meaning being filled with spirit, being in-spired, en-theos – filled with the Divine – then there is no dispiritedness, and no room for disease, and illness, which are invasive forces, to enter.

Typically we experience soul loss as a result of a severe trauma. A part of our vital nature goes into hiding so that we can survive what is happening. So in a time of extreme stress, in order for the whole self to survive, a soul fragment leaves. This is a natural survival mechanism which helps at the time but then needs attention in later life if we want to become whole again.

In the shamanic way of seeing the world, there is no such thing as linear time. You saw on the medicine wheel (Chapter 2) that the body exists in the present moment (west). Emotions are about the past, and the mind plans the future, but the body exists only now. Memory is stored in the body, so whatever happened in the past is, in that sense, still happening somewhere now. The shaman can therefore journey to that place, find out what happened, and bring back the lost soul part and the life-force it contains.

The soul-retrieval journey

The journey for soul retrieval is similar to the power-animal journey described before. It involves going down the tunnel to the Lowerworld, connecting with your power animal and any other helpers one may develop as you gain experience, and then journeying to the Lowerworld of the client. Sometimes, as before, a side tunnel will appear off your tunnel which will lead directly there. The power animal or helper will then lead you to the place where the soul fragment is. The fragment, which is often in a state of distress, appears as a younger version of the client, and may not be at all happy to come back so that a negotiation will have to take place to prove it is now safe to return. It is then a case of bringing back the soul part and blowing the life-force back into the client. This creates an energy change which takes from three days to about two weeks to fully integrate, and the client may well benefit from some form of support or therapy while the change is taking place.

The soul fragment departed for good reason. It is not going to stay around if those reasons are still valid. Soul retrieval brings about a great opportunity to change but we still have to do the work to integrate that change into our lives. Buried memories and emotions, often uncomfortable, will resurface after soul retrieval. This is a sign that healing is taking place. It is good to remember that in all deep-level healing, things get worse before they get better. The pus in the wound must come out before the wound heals or the healing will not work.

Soul retrieval is therapeutic but is is not therapy. However, it is a great help at times such as when the therapeutic process is stalled, as it can bring a magical change to a person's inner energy. It is good to have support after soul retrieval so one uses the great opportunity of having that life-force returned. A therapist can only work with the parts of a person which are actually there. Soul retrieval can bring missing parts back and hence assist the therapeutic process considerably.

Examples of soul retrievals

Some years ago at The Skyros Centre on the splendid Greek island of the same name, I was asked by a participant in a workshop I was conducting to do a soul retrieval for her. Tracy explained she had what felt like old memories that were just outside consciousness and would not quite surface. They were troubling her and she just could not deal with them, and it felt as if this was draining her energy.

We lay down side by side in the customary way and I turned on the drumming tape. Almost as soon as I entered the tunnel, Eagle came and guided me to a different landscape from my familiar one. We went first of all into a valley with forbidding mountains either side.

It was a place of quite lush vegetation yet not a welcoming place. There was a stream running between the mountains and as I journeyed on following Eagle, the valley narrowed and the mountains, now even more forbidding, came closer together. The overall feeling was now of considerable threat and darkness.

Quite suddenly we came out on to a beach and went on toward the sea. The weather was atrocious and dark. Out in the bay was an old sailing ship of the Elizabethan period. I was guided there, and then taken below decks into the belly of the ship, a very dark and dank place. I went through dark and threatening narrow passages with cabin doors either side, again I had the feeling of darkness and threat. Then I turned a sharp corner, went through a door and suddenly found myself in the living room of what felt like a small terraced house of the type on many housing estates. In the corner was a girl of about four years old or so looking very miserable, neglected and bored and tearing paper into strips just for something to do. Her mother was sitting at a table, bored and uninterested, and then her father entered, furiously angry like a dark cloud, and her parents started arguing. It felt that this was a regular occurrence. The girl felt alone, miserable and unloved. It was indicated to me that I was to bring her back. I asked her and she shrugged – might as well I suppose. I assured her that things were different now and she would be welcomed. She came, reluctantly at first, and I brought her back and blew her energy into Tracy's chest and the fontanelle at the top of her head.

When I described the journey in full and came to the last part, Tracy exclaimed 'I remember when that was'. It seems that was the moment when her parents finally broke up. She had been left to live with her mother feeling very unwanted, and part of her had become stuck in that feeling of doubt and worthlessness, and, of course, inexpressable rage which was where her energy was leaking to.

She had lost a big part of herself there. Now the energy was beginning to be returned.

Here is a soul-retrieval journey my friend and co-worker Alison Lees did on behalf of a client:

Linda called me to ask if I could help her young son of four, Jason. His father and he were at loggerheads. He was very clingy and could be quite hyperactive. There were certainly other difficulties that were having a negative effect on him, especially that Linda and the boy's father did not get on any longer and she felt they were only together because of Jason.

From a shamanic perspective everyone in this situation is affected. Linda also told me that she felt as if Jason had not fully incarnated when he was born and that meant he was not really fully here in this life. She also felt that he was somehow being held in the past and was having difficulty growing up to his age. I told her that I would have a look by doing a shamanic journey and finding out what healing he needed.

Linda had brought her mother along to babysit Jason but this was not to be, as Jason insisted on being there when I spoke with her. She had to tell me in a hushed voice how Jason was badly affected by his father. After we had spoken, I asked them both to go out of the room while I journeyed alone to ask what the healing was and how to proceed. I usually do this with the client present but, as he was a child, I felt I needed to do it differently.

The spirits told me that I needed to do a soul retrieval, to cut some ties between Jason and his mother and to find a symbol for her. All of them needed to be there and I needed to give the grandmother a stone to hold and to tell her that she was a very important part of this and her role was to be a rock. The spirits' main advice was to 'just do it as if you are on a train'. This was a little confusing but I did as I was told.

When they came back into the room, I asked Jason if he liked trains, 'Does he like trains?' his mother replied. 'They are his passion at the moment!' So I said that we were going on a train journey and he and I were going to be at the front of the train and his mum and grandma would be in the carriages behind us. To my delight and without any more prompting, the two women took their places on the train. I gave the grandmother the stone, saying to her what the spirits told me to say. Jason and I went to sit down at the front of the train in the driving compartment. I told him I would drive the train and he could hold my hand. I would in fact be shaking the rattle in order to put myself into an altered state and go into the journey. This hyperactive little boy gently and quietly sat down beside me and put out his hand for me to hold. I told him that he could stay with me or he could at any time go and visit his mum or grandma behind, but he needed to do it quietly.

So, I held his hand and off we went. I started to rattle and I stated the intention of the journey, which was to find the soul part that would help Jason. I entered the tunnel and went down. Right away I was taken to a dark high place and within the walls were tombs. I saw a young man of about 30 cocooned in the rocks. There was a sense of fear and numbness. This was Jason as if in the future with a message for the present. I brought him out of that place and we left and went to a healing tree. This soul part, once recovered, brought 'groundedness' and 'solidity'. I asked the spirits if there were others, and I was told to go to the pool, and inside was a newborn Jason. This part was returning 'freshness'. I usually find out much more information when a soul retrieval is done but here it did not matter so much as it was far more 'immediate' as he was so young. I brought back the soul part and blew it in for him.

We took a break then for a cup of tea. (After all, this is England.) We returned to the room for the second part of the healing which was to 'cut the ties'. Without me asking or saying a thing Jason turned over, exposing his back to me in the exact place I needed to work. I was able to release him from the ties he did not need and so return energy to his mother. I then needed, as part of the same process, to journey for a symbol for her, and within a stark, cold, windy landscape a red, juicy ball of energy was brought back. 'Warmth in a cold climate' was the message, but I was also shown a Douglas Fir tree. The teaching from this was for her to spend time with trees and to learn from them. I returned this energy to her by blowing it into her heart. We completed with each of them blowing out a candle.

As they were leaving to go home, the grandmother came up to me and said, 'Thank you for my stone. It's a timely reminder and I need it right now.' I told Linda that she needed to have some work done too, with me or with others, as that would also have a beneficial effect on the family. She reported a week or so later that Jason was getting on really well with his father and things were a lot calmer. She came to see me a few weeks later and, prior to coming, I asked her to request a healing dream. She told me that the night before she came she woke up from a very powerful dream which she could not remember and said to herself, 'Was that it?' Then in his sleep, lying next to her, her son Jason called out, 'Mummy, I'm on the train.'

This was particularly satisfying because after seeing Jason and Linda I later saw the grandmother and her other grandson.

CHAPTER 7

Stopping the World

Ceremonies and Quests

WE HUMANS succeed best in the process of healing and balancing ourselves if we embrace the two modalities at once – the Red Road and the Blue Road. The one being the process of 'erasing our personal history' by seeing our robotic self for what it is and our mass of inherited beliefs for what they are, and the other being a path of extending our consciousness through contact with other worlds than the three-dimensional world of everyday. To contact other worlds we need to 'stop' the processes of the everyday mind from dominating our existence. This is not easy, and in this chapter we are going to look at some methods starting with perhaps the oldest – ceremony.

Ceremony demands that we stop what we are doing and enter into a symbolic enactment. This enactment will mark some change, and while in the ceremony, time and space have different meanings, tomorrow's anxieties are put away for the duration, past pains and joys are in abeyance. All that matters is the ceremony and everything in the ceremony is present right here and now. Ego dominance gets a rest along with busy-busyness and getting and going, must-ing and ought-ing, trying and succeeding or failing, as none of those concepts apply in sacred space and time.

A deeply moving ceremony, where spirit is invoked and the setting is clearly directed towards a purpose greater than everyday concerns, brings all participants into a higher place of consciousness within themselves. One such ceremony is the sweatlodge. The sweatlodge is the forerunner of all steam baths, saunas and all such treatments, in fact they all are secular versions of a spiritual ceremony of purification, of thanksgiving to the earth, and of making prayers to creation.

Sweatlodge ceremony

The sweatlodge is probably the most ancient way of purification known to humans on the planet. In the sweatlodge one is cleansed and purified physically, emotionally, mentally and spiritually. While the sauna is a derivative of the sweatlodge of the ancient Scandinavian peoples, the most familiar sweatlodge in the West today is in the style of the plains Native Americans. It is constructed out of saplings bent and tied together to form an upside-down shape like a saucer or half sphere. This frame is then covered with blankets, tarpaulins and whatever is available until it is dark inside and sufficiently well covered to keep the heat in.

A fire is built outside the lodge, typically about 2 metres (10–15 feet) away, usually to the east, in a special way. A base is laid of slow-burning logs, typically about 15–20cm (5–8 inches) in diameter, and then kindling and small pieces of dry wood are laid on top to form a flat surface. The rocks, which need to be volcanic to withstand the heat, are laid in a cone shape on top. A nice way to do this is to involve everyone who is to sweat to join together and place the rocks on the fire in turn while saying a prayer.

Around this cone of rocks is placed more wood to cover the rocks and provide a draw to pull the fire up from the base. It takes about an hour and a half for the rocks to heat, by which time the fire is burnt down from the cone shape and the rocks have fallen through the base and can be removed. The participants create an altar outside the lodge door on the east side. A 'spirit trail' is laid connecting the fire to the altar and then to the pit for the hot rocks which has been dug in the centre of the lodge.

The lodge chief traditionally enters the lodge first to 'bless and awaken' it with sage and cedar and sometimes with the sacred pipe, to pray and invoke the powers of the four directions for the healing of the participants. When all is ready the people line up beside the spirit trail and are smudged with sage and cedar incense prior to entering the lodge. The door is always made low so one crawls in on all fours, and it is traditional to make a prayer on entering such as 'For all my relations', or in native language, *'omitakuaye oyasin'*. The meaning here is that I sweat not just for myself but for all to whom I am related – which is all of creation. By purifying and healing myself I affect all things for the better. The sweatlodge is seen as the womb of Mother Earth, and the ceremony is one of entering the darkness, purifying, healing – becoming more whole, dying a little – and then coming out at the end cleansed and reborn.

The people sit around the central pit, close together in a small space. The rocks are brought in and blessed with sage, firstly seven rocks symbolising the four directions of the manifest world plus the above, the below, and finally the creator/creation. Further stones are then brought in until there is enough to give the required heat. In some traditions this is a very specific number, but in practice the chief adjusts it according to the number needed for the temperature to be right. The door is closed when everyone is ready, and the chief calls in the powers, making an offering of water to the rocks at the end of each prayer.

There are a many forms for a sweatlodge. In many of the lodges I have participated in, the first round of prayers is for oneself. It is considered important to start with oneself as until one is healed and in balance, anything one attempts to do for others will be tainted with one's own needs and imbalances. The people pray one by one in turn in a sunwise (or clockwise) circle. At the end of a prayer it is traditional to say, 'Ho! I have spoken' and then the chief puts an offering of water on the rocks to carry the prayer in the steam to the spirit world, and then the next person takes their turn. At the end of the prayers, often a chant or two will be sung, and then the 'round' ends, the door is opened and drinking water is passed to the participants. More red-hot, glowing rocks will then be brought in and then the second round begins. The prayer this time is for anything and anybody except oneself.

The same procedure continues with the third round which is prayers for the 'giveaway'. This is an opportunity to make prayers to let go of aspects of oneself that no longer serve the highest good, and also to offer one's gifts and talents in service of spirit. The fourth round has no set form, as now we have prayed it is time to listen. Hence it might be a silent meditation, a journey to the land of the power animals, or a time of chanting or toning together or something else that feels appropriate to the chief in the moment. At the end the chief gives thanks to the powers, often pours rather a lot of water on the rocks until the lodge is decidedly hot, and finally the door is opened and we come out looking pink and sweaty and dive into the water if there is a nearby stream, or lie on the ground.

In the words of Stalking Wolf, the Apache Grandfather who taught Tom Brown and is immortalised in Tom's books *The Vision*, *The Quest* and *Grandfather*:

> You have felt the presence of the ancients, the expansion of self, and the peace. You know now what a true ceremony should be, for as you felt the power of the lodge, so too will others, regardless of belief. The sweatlodge speaks to all peoples in the language of their own beliefs and thus it becomes a universal truth. So, then, use the lodge as a tool, a doorway for physical and spiritual renewal and cleansing, a pathway to expansion and a vehicle to the worlds of the unseen and eternal.

In the words of Ed McGaa Eagleman: 'While the sweatlodge itself is simple to describe, it is beyond any mortal writer's ability to adequately convey the ultimate culmination of spiritual, mystical and psychic expression of the sweatlodge ceremony. You have to experience it to truly realise its fullness and depth ...' I have been asked numerous times by people who have never entered a sweatlodge, 'What is the difference between a sauna or Turkish bath and a sweatlodge ceremony?' My answer is that there is almost nothing similar except for heat and sweat. I have had this view confirmed by many first timers at the end of their first sweatlodge.

Ceremonies for fear, anger and grief

Fear sits on the medicine wheel in the south with the element of water. A good way to work with fear is to give your fears to the water. Running water – a stream or river – is really good for this. One can 'see' the fears going with the flow of the water. When you feel complete, give thanks to the water.

Anger sits on the west of the wheel with the element of earth. A good way to work with anger is the one that Chippewa medicine man Sun Bear used to teach. Go into nature, somewhere you can be alone, and take a tool with you so you can dig a hole. When you have your hole ready, pour your anger, rage, bitterness and so on into it. Give it to the earth, the Mother can take it and transform it. Pour your heart's pain out. Let whatever is stuck in there be exorcised. When you feel complete, or as complete as you can for the present, knowing you can return another day, cover the hole with earth, give thanks, and leave without looking back.

Grief is such an endemic part of life – along with joy – I am unable to place it in any one direction of the wheel. I can find it in all directions. A couple of years ago I attended a workshop lead by Malidoma Somé and his wife Sobonfu who are African shamans of the Dagara tribe of Burkina Faso. They took us through an African village-style grief ritual, a deeply moving and very beautiful ceremony. We, the 80 or so group members, created a most beautiful altar out of natural things which we placed at one end of a grass meadow while at the other end we set up 'the village', a space of gathering and mingling. The ceremony began in the evening and went on well into the night with the drums playing and the group singing an ongoing chant for many hours. When anyone was moved to grief, they left the 'village' and went to the altar to express whatever was in their soul. While they did this another group member spontaneously followed them as quiet support in case of need.

As the ceremony went on much grief, and rage too, was expressed, and a great exorcism and clearing took place. The following day there was a feeling of greater presence amongst all who had participated, eyes were brighter, hearts were lighter and there was a sense of release of baggage and of greater energy available for life.

EXERCISE

To work with grief on your own, make a 'giveaway' out of nature, a bundle of beauty into which you put your feelings. Place it on your altar at home or in a suitable place where you can go and commune with it. Allow yourself to be moved to release your grief into the bundle. When you feel complete – or as complete as you can for now – give the bundle away into water, spread it on the earth, or if it feels right, ceremonially burn it. Whatever you do, make it a ceremony and give thanks for the release.

Trees

In this land of cities, concrete and technology it is so easy to forget we live on the Earth, we are part of the Earth, the Earth created us and we belong to the Earth. One of the most pernicious errors in thinking is the extraordinary idea that the Earth belongs to us. Somewhere in the Bible is the phrase that God put us on the Earth to have 'dominion' over it. What a lot of deadly confusion that statement has caused.

Our bodies are made from the Earth, everyday we eat the products of the Earth in order to live, we breath the atmosphere of the Earth, we defecate back to the Earth – waste products of one type of being are food for another – we depend totally on the other kingdoms of the Earth for our livelihood. Without the humble garden worm doing its magic to the soil, we would starve.

As the trees breathe out, we breathe in. Horrendous amounts of the rainforests are being cut down. The rainforests are the lungs of the Earth. Without the lungs of the Earth, our lungs will not have enough to breathe. Trees are a key to life. When journeying to assist deceased human spirits who are stuck between the worlds, we tend to find them near trees. Trees are of great importance to life.

EXERCISE

◆ Go out and find a tree that you like and feel good around. All trees are not necessarily keen on humans (understandably) so it is good to feel around to be sure you find one that welcomes you. Sit with the tree and ask for its wisdom. We have done a tree ceremony earlier in this book and here is another one.

◆ Find four stones. Lay your four stones in the four cardinal directions around the tree. Sit with your back to the tree and first of all:

1. Face south (water, emotions, past) and ask, 'How do I feel now at the deepest place inside me?'

2. Face north (air, mind, future) and ask, 'What is my true direction, my path, what does my highest self seek to make manifest?'

3. Face west (earth, body, present moment) and ask, 'How does my body feel, what are its needs, what does Mother Earth call me to do?'

4. Face east (fire, spirit, timelessness) and ask, 'For what service has Spirit given birth to me?'

◆ Then change your position and:

1. Sit in the south and face the tree to your north. Ask, 'What must I giveaway to balance my emotional life?'

2. Sit in the north facing a tree to your south. Ask, 'What must I giveaway for clarity of mind?'

3. Sit in the west facing the tree to your east. Ask, 'What must I give up to heal my body completely?'

4. Sit in the east facing the tree to your west. Ask, 'What must I giveaway to find my path with heart?'

When complete, make a small offering and give thanks. Find a quiet, comfortable place and write your insights and any messages received in your journal.

Vision quest

One of the most profound, ancient ceremonies is the vision quest. It has been so since before recorded time. Buddha is said to have sat under the Bodhi Tree until he became enlightened. In the Bible, Jesus is reported as vision questing for 40 days and 40 nights. In the West, Steven Foster and Meredith Little have pioneered the vision quest for urban and suburban people and have done much wonderful work with both adults and teenagers. They wrote *The Book of The Vision Quest*, a magical treatise which I have used time and again when conducting visions quests in Wales.

The traditional vision quest of many peoples is three or four days and nights alone and fasting in nature. It has three distinct parts the first of which is *severance* when you prepare yourself and open your inner structures of being, when you look at your addictions, your joys and sorrows, grief and anger, love and compassion. Fear is a companion at this time. It needs to be there, as an ally and friend it keeps you alert. Much of your subsequent experience will depend upon the quality of preparation. You learn a lot on a vision quest about the value of preparation and about how much you actually care for and love yourself. Preparation is an act of self-love and later you will reap the rewards or otherwise of the quality of your self-care at this time.

The next stage is *threshold*. This is when you leave the everyday behind and enter sacred time and place. There is just you and the natural world. No house, no central heating, no electricity, no switches, no traffic, no telephones, no lunchtime, no dinnertime, nothing to feed your addictions, no other person's needs to be fulfilled, no excuses to make, just you and yourself and the timeless eternity of Mother Earth and her kingdoms. You watch the stately progress of the Sun, the Moon, the stars; the little animals and birds scurry around doing their things, looking at you, the interloper in what they consider to be their territory; you hear the inner dialogue going on inside your head and gradually you begin to wonder who you really are and what you are doing on earth and why. Perhaps on the second day you begin to pay attention to the emptiness, to eternity, to existence itself rather than your anxieties about it. At some stage it may dawn on you that you really are alone not just at this moment but at all moments, and that you stand and fall by your own actions. You create your reality out of what is available, you are responsible for your life, you are the creator of what you have, it is your game you are playing, you are nobody's slave except your own. Yet you are part of All-That-Is, a part of everything around you, so in another way of seeing and feeling, you are not alone at all.

Everything that happens is part of the quest. One time in Wales, a participant came back to the camp in tears about half an hour into her quest. She had dropped her sleeping bag (necessary equipment in Wales) and it had rolled into the river and got soaked, and she did not know what to do. I reminded her this was part of her quest, found her another one and she went back to her place. In telling her story afterwards the incident reflected many occurrences in her life and illustrated something valuable about how she handled setbacks and how she could do it differently.

The final stage is *reincorporation*, the return to the everyday. One returns, tired and hungry, and there is tea and porridge, warmth and comfort. Yet one returns to a changed world which will only reveal itself slowly, piece by piece. Then there is the telling of the stories, the hero's and heroine's journeys, the experiences. This is so valuable because we are all part of one. A group of questers quest for themselves but also in a subtle way for each other. In telling one's own story, much that might seem disjointed or even irrelevant starts to make sense, and in hearing the others' stories, one's own can be seen and felt from a much wider perspective.

Some years ago a participant, a dourly inclined Scotsman, came back from a short quest angrily declaiming 'that was 23 hours and 59 minutes of total waste of time'. I am not sure his language wasn't rather more colourful. The next day, late on in the reincorporation phase, he had his turn to tell his story. After hearing many other stories, he found a lot of value in his own experience and that it had no longer been a waste of time at all, but rather a highly illuminating experience.

The following year Andy Raven, one of my co-workers, and I were conducting a three-day vision quest and at the first meeting I told that story to illustrate that the value of this work is not always obvious. I had quite forgotten who the story was about until a voice the other side of the tipi said, 'That was me.' He had come back for more.

Vision quests affect lives for a long time. After a quest, one's life, friends and culture can look and feel different and one may be moved to make changes unthought of before. Looking back, a quest can be seen as a marker, a moment after which things were never quite the same.

After any profound experience of potential great change, there tends to be a time of reversal when all the old demons and habits get together and say something like, 'So you think you changed? So you think you actually achieved something? You really think you got rid of us? Who do you think you are?' A feeling of depression and loss of energy can come upon one. This is the enemy of inertia – deadness – of the west direction of the medicine wheel. All the old patterns come out, the old habits, the old robotic behaviours, the old addictions, and then energy can be lost in the inner conflict between the old you and the new you which is in the process of birthing. You have a very important task to stay on the side that you want to win the battle.

I frequently watch this battle going on within participants on courses I lead, and it is my job to lend my weight to assist the part of the person which is seeking freedom. I must never interfere, only assist, or it becomes my work not theirs. Most times freedom wins but sometimes I watch helplessly, as the enemy within takes over and rejects the budding transformation. Sometimes I have suddenly found myself the 'bad guy' as I then represent the part of them-self they are rejecting. No one can do another's work and no one has the right to do another's work. The line between assisting others and interfering in their process is extremely thin, but must be observed by all practitioners at all times.

The full benefit of a vision quest and any profound ceremony comes after the old demons have returned for their final attack and been vanquished. It is by weathering this storm and staying strong and firmly on the side of the part of you that confronts the natural fear of change and dares to renew yourself, that you really incorporate the change within. Wrestle the old dragons and demons, wrestle them to the ground. When you have done so they will grin and say, 'Well done' and become your allies. A habit defeated, a robotic behaviour conquered, an addiction vanquished, becomes a friend for life, an inner strength.

One participant commented sometime after her quest:

> I am much more in touch with my power and balance and have a stronger sense of self. During my vision quest I battled for hours with my needs versus what people think of me/their expectations of me, and probably for the first time in my life, my needs won. The quest was the beginning of my step into true adulthood, finding my power within, which is something for an independent 34-year-old. It was followed by the first major decision of my life which I have not sounded out with or sought an opinion from (and in effect asked permission of) my mother.

Urban vision quest

This is a variation on the above and is suitable for urban dwellers.

EXERCISE

CITY VISION QUEST

◆ Severance. Put aside a day for nothing else but your quest. Prepare yourself, wear suitable clothing – perhaps even special clothing to help put you in sacred space – gather all you need, get ready. Meditate on your intent for the quest, on the most important things in your life you would like guidance on.

◆ Threshold. Your front door is your threshold. Place something of note above or around your door to mark your movement into sacred time. Meditate at the threshold and, when ready, move through, knowing that you are now entering sacred time-space until you return. Everything that happens is part of your quest, however ordinary or bizarre it might be.

◆ Choose a starting point in the city and proceed there. From your starting point.

◆ Walk towards the east, hold the personal intent of your quest as background and ask the question, 'Who Am I?' Follow any spontaneous nudges, notice anything that happens, especially anything that seems in any way unusual. Be aware of your surroundings at all times. You are in the magical world and at any time it might send you a message.

◆ Ask for illumination on your existence. Why has spirit given birth to you? How are you here to serve?

◆ When you feel you are answered or at least moved to 'see' something that you did not before, take a moment to sit and write in your journal.

◆ Then walk south with the same intent and ask the question, 'What are the gifts and burdens from my past?' Look into your past. What formed you, what influences moved you, whose dreams were you asked to be? What are your own personal dreams now and are you manifesting them?

◆ Again when you have a sense of being answered, take a rest and write down your insights.

◆ Walk in the direction of the west with the question, 'Why am I here on earth?' In this, the only moment of power, ask, 'Why am I here in existence? Who am I now and where is the power? What am I serving?'

◆ Lastly walk towards the north and ask, 'Where Am I Going? Am I actually going where I really wish to go?' The adult part of ourself needs to have a road map. Ask, 'How much of my path is my spirit's choice and how much is it external factors, automatic behaviours, old beliefs and habits that are pushing me?'

◆ Finally return home, ceremonially re-enter through your threshold, and begin reincorporation. Take down anything you put up on your door – it is now just a door. After refreshment, sit quietly and feel into the whole experience of your day. What has it reflected of your self and your life?

Disrupting routines

A very good exercise for awareness is to change consciously and systematically your habitual routines. Make a list of regular habits such as the routes you use for particular journeys, your mealtimes and eating habits, moments when addictions make themselves known. Drinkers and smokers very often have regular times of day when alcohol or tobacco demand their attention. One could put that another way and say that at certain times of day alcohol and tobacco 'steal power' from their addicts. Television steals power from lots of people from about 7 p.m. in the evening.

EXERCISE

Are there habits, routines, indulgences, addictions that steal your power? Take a look and make a list. Look for regularities in your life that you can change. List them and set about changing one at a time. See what difference it makes to your degree of awakeness.

Experiencing the shadows

Most of the time we habitually look at objects. Instead, for, say, the next two weeks, look at the shadows in-between the objects. Reverse your foreground-background perspective. Try to see the background as foreground, view the shadows as the primary objects and the objects as the shadows. Practise with trees and their leaves first and then go on to other things until you can do it with everything. (Take a break when driving a car!)

Enjoying silence

Particularly if one lives in a city or busy conurbation, there is a lot of constant noise. Try reducing the noise in your life. If you constantly play music, give it a break. Instead listen to the spaces, the silences, the voids in the sounds around you. Listen to the spaces between footsteps, between words spoken to you, hear the quiet hum of existence.

Gazing

Take a time of quiet and just gaze. Let the shadows and the silence speak to you. Let your eyes be unfocussed and gaze 'through' objects. This is an exercise in 'not-doing' and is a challenge to the active mind. So listen to the stuff of mind while you do this, the inner dialogue that moseys on and on, the rattle of the ego's fear.

In normal consciousness we see only a small spectrum of the light frequencies and we hear only a small range of audio frequencies. We do not see ultra violet and infra red, we do not hear dog whistles, our normal senses are severely limited. Let yourself gaze, and while you do let your body quieten and your breathing get slower and slower. If a mantra helps try repeating something like, 'I am alive and gazing. I see beyond.'

Knocks of the spirit

Nudges, hunches, omens, odd happenings, weird feelings, these are all ways the spirit – the non-manifest world – contacts us. Synchronicities, and seeming coincidences are all indications of a connection and a possible message or reminder from the other side of life. Most of us lead very busy, programmed lives and so being available for the nudge of spirit is difficult. One could even say that the way most of us tend to live our lives is like a defence against the possible knocks of spirit. Pity. Being available is a precursor for hearing spirit's messages. At least we can take quiet times to make ourselves available. Meditation times.

Altar

It is a really good idea to create your own personal altar somewhere at home. An altar is to remind you of your origins in the spirit world and that life is more than the three-dimensional experience. One way to make your altar is to start with a piece of cloth, a few objects and a candle. The objects are to remind you of magic moments when you 'just knew', those amazing times of power when the matrix reveals a bit of itself and we are uplifted. When you gaze at your altar it helps pull you to a higher, more connected state of consciousness, to a feeling of connection to the source.

Incense

Incense has been used in cultures all over the world since before recorded time. Burning incense brings beautiful odours and a feeling of purification to the space you are in, and also puts out a call to higher consciousness. Scientifically, burning herbs has been shown to encourage the presence of negative ions – these are the positive ones that make you feel good, such as around flowing water or at the edge of the sea – and banish positive ions which are the negative ones, such as those around electric trains and pylons that make you feel drowsy and down.

Burning incense – smudging is an alternative term – at the start of a ceremony brings people to enter sacred space and a state of quietness. It encourages a light 'trance' state in which the busy mind is more still and one is more receptive to the nudges of spirit and more connected to earth and existence.

Making a sigil

This is a way of creating a design which incorporates the essence of what you wish to draw into your life. One sigil for one item. First you need to be very clear about what you are asking for. This is extremely necessary as you are very likely to get what you want. If you have not been rigorously clear, it may well not be quite the outcome you intended.

EXERCISE

♦ Sit quietly and write about what you wish to bring into your life. 'More money' is no good at all. Name your price specifically but remember the difference between need and greed. Remember what happens to many lottery winners – vast sums tend to ruin lives. And also asking spirit for what you need for a better life is quite different to asking spirit to fulfil your greed and indulgence. There is something too about asking for what will enable you to assist in the evolution of the collective – to make an effective giveaway that is of benefit to all – rather than just divert wealth to you for personal gain. Having a spiritual purpose is to have a purpose that fulfils something of value to the greater whole while bringing you pleasure and joy too.

♦ Write down clearly something you wish to bring into your life. Define it with great care. Simplify it down to the essentials, being sure you really have got it just right. Then look at what you have in front of you – a string of letters forming words, is what they are in essence: symbols. Cross out all the letters repeated more than once and look at the shapes you have left. Now form these shapes into one shape in such a way that the essence of each shape is included. You only need the shapes once – for example if you have an R, that includes the shape of a P; if you have an M, that is a W upside down, so there is no need to put in anything else.

♦ Now create the sigil – that is what you now have – into a pleasing artistic sign. Bless it, make a ceremony to empower it, bathe it in incense, and then hang it on your wall. It will act as a point of focus and a magical talisman to attract towards you what you have encapsulated into it.

Fire ceremony

The fire ceremony is a giveaway ceremony and is for releasing that of yourself which no longer serves you. It is a ceremony of transformation, and fire is both literally and metaphysically the great element of change. The effectiveness of the fire ceremony, like everything else in shamanism – and life, because shamanism is about keys to life – is intent and the degree of focus put into the intent. A slipshod ceremony is not worth bothering with – just like a slipshod anything. A ceremony requires your full focus and intention, participation, commitment and will for it to be effective. It also depends on your beliefs – not so much about your belief as to whether ceremony is effective, but your beliefs about whether *you* are worthy and that you deserve the effects of the change you are seeking to make. Take a look inside at yourself and your beliefs. Remember your innate worth, that you are a valued and necessary part of creation – why else would you have been created?

The mythology of the fire ceremony says that whatever you truly, unconditionally give away, release, let go of into Grandfather Fire, then spirit will return to you that which spirit wills to be for you tenfold, and what spirit wills is not to be yours will be released for ever.

As with just about all things in life, there are two sides to the fire ceremony. The one is to focus on releasing that which no longer serves you, the garbage you have been carrying, the burdens, habits, robotic behaviours, addictions, dependencies, judgments, expectancies, neediness and so on, and the other is to call to you that which you really want to make manifest in your life, your most precious dreams, desires, wishes and hopes. Whatever you pray for in a fire ceremony needs to be prayed for without attachment to the outcome. Do your best, speak your truth, pray with an open heart, shout and scream if needs be with all the energy at your disposal, and then let it go. Spirit will return tenfold what is for you, and the rest you have already given away. So you can win but you cannot lose.

A good way to encapsulate the energy is to make two offerings, one of each energy. They can be as simple as a piece of paper with our feelings written on them to something sculpted out of bits and pieces from nature. One traditional way is to make prayer arrows, a straight one for the giveaway of your gifts and talents and a bent one for the baggage you seek to release. Find a straight and a bent stick of wood. Make the straight piece beautiful, perhaps by winding coloured wool around it in a pleasing pattern. You can put your written offering under the wool so your feelings are there in the arrow. Make the bent one in such a way that it suits what you are releasing and it contains the feelings you have. Just one point that is important to remember: everything you seek to let go of has been there with you for a purpose. You may not have liked it but it has brought you experience and growth, so let it go with thanks not with anger. If you think about it, it is impossible to let anything go with anger because if you are holding anger you are not letting go.

To enact the ceremony you first of all need a fire. This can be anything from a real live fire to a simple candle, though a real fire, especially out in nature, brings one to a much closer feeling of connection with the elements and the earth. First it is good to smudge yourself and anyone else taking part. Then call to the powers of the four directions with special emphasis on the spirit of fire, and the above and below and the Creator. Singing a chant or two brings a good feeling and gives you time to come into harmony and balance, and enter into sacred space and time.

It is good next to make an offering to the fire. Traditional offerings are tobacco, essential oil, chocolate (Mexican tradition), rice or grains, but anything that feels good to you will be all right. Ask Grandfather Fire to accept your offerings and transform the energy contained in them. The ceremony is a way of passing a message from the world of everyday to the world of non-manifest energy or spirit. If you work with the medicine wheel teachings, that means from west to east. To make your giveaway, place yourself to the west of the fire, offer your giveaway with prayers and watch it burn up completely. Then pass your hands through Grandfather Fire and bring the energy of fire to your third eye, then to your heart and then to your *hara* – solar plexus area. This enacts bringing the divine flame to your spirit, your heart and your body-mind. On completion give thanks to the spirit world and to fire.

On my first trip to Peru in the 1980s, the Inca shaman don Eduardo Calderon took the group I was part of through the fire ceremony – and much else – and he said it is a really good ceremony to do every full moon. He suggested doing it for 13 moons after we got back home. I obediently did so and have been doing it on the full moon ever since with very few misses. That is for about 15 years. I reckon that was the idea. Typical shamanic trickery.

CHAPTER 8

Trance-dance

Gateway to ecstasy

DANCE IS ONE OF THE MOST MOVING, transformative and beautiful paths I know, and it combines celebration, self-expression, moving past ego, healing old trauma, entering realms of pure energy, touching raw power, connecting with that wonderful place where there is nothing to do but laugh. Yes, it can be a whole heap of joy.

Traditional societies all over the world dance. They dance to celebrate, to bring their society together and they dance to enter the spirit worlds and receive guidance and help. Dance is as important a gateway to the spirit worlds for traditional shamans as is the shamanic journey described in Chapter 5. In fact there is little difference other than one is in movement and the other supine. One can dance to find and retrieve a power animal as an alternative to journeying.

The Tungus people of Siberia (where the word shaman comes from) dance to travel to the Upper and Lowerworlds. To travel to the Lowerworld the shaman will call his reindeer helper and engage in a complex dance to embody the process of the journey. And yes – shades of Father Christmas whose earliest origins come from these northern lands where the reindeer was considered a valuable spirit helper as well as a practical everyday assistant.

The !Kung bushmen of South Africa dance to channel a healing power they call !Num which comes to the dancers as a boiling heat. It seems that initially the dance is agony but as they come to harmonise with the power, it becomes ecstatic and they can bring the power to the sick and heal with it.

155

West African traditions have used dance since before recorded time and many traditions have their origins there such as the Gnawas of Morocco and the Candomble and Umbanda of Brazil – more about them in a moment.

Another dance form is the Sun Dance as practised by the Lakota and other Native North American nations. This is a community prayer dance which usually goes on for three or four days and involves considerable sacrifice by the participants. It is a dance of thanksgiving for being alive and is also a search for personal and community vision in which the dancers push themselves beyond ordinary physical limits into an altered ecstatic state in which the difference between the everyday and the spirit world disappear.

Another Native American dance is known as the Long Dance. It is a ceremonial dance in which the participants usually dance in a sunwise circle, often around a fire, and which goes on a long time, such as dusk till dawn. I have participated in many British versions of this and found them to be wondrous, uplifting, celebratory, energy moving and sometimes transcendental happenings. Like a hiker getting to second wind, one has to dance through the pain threshold until the dance begins to do the dancing, and the barriers of self and energy melt and the space begins to move around the still point of oneself. Then existence is and 'self' is just a concept of a part of that all-embracing, throbbing, vital existence that is the dance of life.

It seems that in Europe the Tarantella was a form of trance-dance in which the participants would shake and tremble. Then there was the group of white Christians in America known as the Shakers who danced and sang and shook, but unfortunately they were infected with such strong anti-sexual ideas that they all died out. More recently there is the wonderful work of Gabrielle Roth, who got me started on the dancing path back in 1978 from which I am more than glad to say I have never looked back.

Power animal dance

Here is an exercise to find and retrieve a power animal which can be done alone, or better still with a group.

EXERCISE

◆ Set up your space and music. Ideally several people with drums and rattles. You can hold a rattle yourself while you do this, to good effect.

◆ Make your hands into fists and begin to move them up and down together in rhythm. Then stomp left, right, left with your feet. Once you get the feeling of the rhythm going through you, call your power animal(s) to come and dance with you and through you. Keep stomping until you feel moved and then turn to your left and begin to move around in a circle. Add your voice and let natural sounds come out – maybe start just with a long note. Animal-like sounds may well want to come through you so encourage them and let what wants to happen happen. There will come a time when the music wants to speed up, and so follow this natural increase in tempo. Let the wild wo/man – the wild animal – express through you, and enjoy the liberation of this part of your nature. Imagine yourself in the jungle, or a natural place, as a part of nature where you can fully let go, where the word 'inhibition' has no currency, and 'shyness' is an absurd idea from a far-off land which the mad inhabit. Revel in the freedom of the nature which is the real you, the wild dancing, singing, expressing being of loving fullness and joy.

In the words of Michael Harner, long-time shamanic teacher and founder of The Centre for Shamanic Studies and author of *The Way Of The Shaman*, 'One thing that usually becomes clear to the dancers is that underneath our ordinary human cultural consciousness is a near-universal emotional connection with wild animal alter egos.'

Trance-dance based on Afro-Brazilian traditions

I have developed a method of trance-dance based loosely on TTT – Terpsichore Trance Therapy – which in turn is based on Afro-Brazilian ways including those of Candomble and Umbanda. A couple of years ago I wrote the following article which appeared in *London and Southeast Connection* magazine. It sums up the essence of trance-dance and later it had a dramatic effect on one person's life, as you will see.

A female dancer wrote to me of her experience at one of my workshops:

> [Saturday] I remember nothing of the trance-dance and was quite surprised when my friend told me I had danced for a long time (over an hour). I thought it was two minutes. I now realise I was dancing the abuse out, no wonder my head was burning. No wonder I was excited. I knew the next day was going to be even more amazing!
>
> [Sunday] This day I will never forget for the rest of my life.
>
> Again in the dance I was gone but I remember coming to and someone had the rain stick near me. I thought if he comes any closer I'll have all his clothes off. Wow! Then this energy was buzzing through me and around me. I stood there thinking, I've got enough sexual energy to make love with every man in this room and start again. It was amazing and exciting. Mine to keep forever
> . . .
>
> Thank you all for making this possible. It was just beautiful, the drumming, the trust, the love and the warmth, the light and the fun. Everything was just as it should be.

A male dancer writes of his experience:

> Trance-dance is an experience of freedom. It is a license to let rip, burn up, freak out, explode and collapse; then post-orgasmically, to re-integrate in the arms of loving companions. When it happens, it

is like plundering a maelstrom of energy . . . I collapse after only a few minutes. But I think it could go on dancing me a whole lot longer, and plenty wilder. Given the opportunity, I would certainly like to push it further. I think I've only been down the nursery slopes. But what I've discovered in these visceral states of only a few minutes has astounded me, altered me.

Underneath my sedate exterior lurks something monstrous, godlike unspeakable. Trance-dance safely uncages it from the 'English reserve'. . . Just a taste of it is a revelation.

He has found the wild man inside himself.

I first encountered the trance-dance in 1984 when I attended the European Association of Humanistic Psychology Conference which took place that year in Guildford, Surrey. One of the sessions was trance-dancing with Dr Jacques Donnars, of Paris, and Professor Arnold Keyserling, of Vienna. They needed music and I supplied them with my ghetto blaster and a tape of Olatunji's *Drums of Passion*.

What I experienced at the session was extraordinary. In quite a short time demure people who one might expect to be shy and inhibited were dancing with wild abandon. Professor Keyserling kept telling me to turn the music up louder and I remember struggling with my player to somehow extract a bit more volume. In those days I was somewhat more inhibited than I am now so I waited some time before trying the dance myself. Finally, I dared to have a go. Jacques told me to keep my eyes closed and then he held my head firmly and turned it around a few times and then spun my whole body. Soon I found myself dancing on a world which seemed to be tilted by about 30 degrees. When I began to fall someone would support me and I spun around in this tilted crazy world dancing wildly until in a moment of panic I blinked my eyes open. The spell was broken as I saw the dirty concrete floor and people's legs.

They called it Terpsichore Trance Therapy, or TTT for short. Terpsichore is the Greek goddess of the dance. This experience made me determined to follow up and learn more and this I was able to do when one of Dr Donnars's trainees came to London and gave a workshop. I then began to experiment with the dance myself and learn more by trial and error.

In the late 1980s I worked with the trance-dance and it helped me find access into more passionate living. It also brought about some transformative moments for workshop participants, yet I felt the need to know more and understand it at a deeper level. In 1992 I went to an international conference on trance and healing in Marrakesh at which 250 people from 25 countries were present, including Dr David Akstein, the founder of TTT, and representatives from the Afro–Brazilian traditions of Candomble and the Umbanda which were his primary-source inspirations. The local Gnawas, who come from the melding of West African and Middle Eastern Sufi traditions, were there too. I had my first experience of their night-long ceremony, the Derdeba, and of their extraordinary trance-inducing music. The conference rekindled my enthusiasm for the whole field of trance-dancing and so-called 'spirit possession' as a path to accessing healing altered states of consciousness and experiences of hidden aspects of self and the universe.

There were many sessions on TTT with Dr Donnars and his son Alain, at which I took the opportunity to enter the dance as many times as possible. There was a wonderful ritual with Carlos Buby of the Umbanda tradition from São Paulo, many other experiential sessions and numerous intellectual discussions on the meaning and value of these ancient ways.

I have worked with the trance-dance since then and found it an amazingly powerful tool. It can move someone who has been stuck and take them into what they need to release quite naturally and without the struggle through 'resistance' usually encountered when working in therapy mode; it can take someone to amazing places of cosmic light and laughter; it can liberate aspects of a person they did not know existed and have not encountered before.

Trance-dancing is almost as old as humanity, nothing could be further from some New Age, new-fangled cure-all fad-therapy. Dancing is natural, the beat of the drum is primal, stomping on the earth is basic to human beingness, rhythm brings order to life. There is a wonderful quote, I forget where from, which says, 'The lords of chaos hate rhythm'! That's right – rhythm helps us into a state of consciousness where the natural laws of the universe are more easily assimilable and where our own true natures come to the surface from beneath whatever repression we live.

We Westerners live under plenty of repression. We are like a nation of control freaks, terrified to let go and let the spirit enter and take us where it will. After all, who knows where that may be? We are forever trying to impose our own conditions upon spirit and say, 'Yes but – I'll change so long as it can be like this – within my known parameters – within my self-chosen limits.' But change means change – it means entering the unknown, and by definition that means the future is not known and cannot be controlled or bargained over. Sorry – spirit will accept no pre-conditions and we cannot know who we will be after the change until we get there.

African traditions, and many other indigenous cultures, have worked with 'spirit possession' for centuries. It sounds scary but if I reframe it as 'ego dispossession', then it is perhaps easier to comprehend. It means having the willingness to enter the unknown where the spirit and not the little ego-mind rules. In our religious history, ego control has become associated with God, and an ordered, rational Apollonian universe full of repressed people has been labelled 'godly', while wild Dionysian letting go, natural uninhibited dancing and drumming, liberation into the realm of unbridled spirit, has got muddled with evil and the devil. It is no wonder this is a hard culture to live in happily. To be a 'normal' person we have to bottle up so much of our self, our spirit.

In this day and age much is happening to help people to greater freedom from the belief systems which brought about the mental, emotional, physical and spiritual slavery of the past. Trance-dancing is a way of reaching back to our ancient indigenous roots in order to help us present-day people touch the freedom of spirit, the right to our own life choices, the passion of life fully lived. Or as the Native Americans might say, to 'dance our dreams awake'.

Here is the story of one person who read that article and was moved to come and dance. The story culminates in experiences of the Trance-dance and in it are many pointers to the kind of pain we can find ourselves living in, and a path that can help us to retrieve ourselves, in spite of a seemingly hopeless situation.

Violet's story

She writes of her background:

'My father was an alcoholic and depressive, my mother over-anxious, dominating and emotionally possessive. The family revolved around my father's illness (presented to me and my siblings as a reaction to the war, not as a pre-existing condition). I was taught that men's desires took precedence over women's, that they were always right, and grew up believing I had nothing worthwhile to say, think or do. Like many children I escaped into a dream world, gaining solace from dreams, visions and talking to trees and animals, although adults tried to control this too.

Her story is one of a desperate, alcoholic, depressive, possessive, domineering family background resulting in feelings of dreadful self-non-worth and a natural striving to escape into a dreamworld. She made various attempts at suicide, got pregnant by mistake at 17, forced into marriage, divorce, depression; a 'clever' GP got her adddicted to Librium, mental hospital, raped in the hospital, self-immolation; married to an alcoholic for 22 years, and so on. She finally made a breakthrough when she began to write successfully and was able to end the marriage and start to do something about her life.

All was far from easy as she felt, 'my shadow selves gathering around me'. This culminated on a course

when we undertook a journey to free our 'wild selves' from our solar plexus. When I 'unzipped' my solar plexus I was knocked backwards off my feet by the ferocity and force of a three-headed demon (large rolling yellow eyes and huge, lolling tongues, and composed of a black, sticky, treacly substance). It came flying out of my solar plexus and, before I could shout, launched itself at me, forcing its way back down my throat (so that I could not speak or breathe), and down my body, splitting itself into snake-like pieces that writhed through every limb, out through every orifice and back in again, raping me over and over until the final dismemberment.

The effect of this journey was shattering. In the weeks that followed I descended to the deepest despair I have ever experienced, to the point where I started to cut myself again. But there was one, vital difference: this time I knew what I was fighting. This thing was real. It manifested around my house, both in its largest, most terrifying form, and as smaller versions, scuttling around in the shadows or gathering at the end of my bed at night. I yelled at my demons, danced for hours and hours to scare them off, and discovered in the process that the trance-like state the dancing achieved did seem to have some effect, though not for long.

Over the following weeks they came and went. I would have days of freedom, and received much healing in the peace of the forest near my home, which they seemed to be unable to enter. Then they would return, either inside me or around the house and the same cycle of great despair and torture, frenzied dancing and sleepless nights would begin again.

Note: one of the big differences between the Western understanding and shamanic understanding of how things are relates to how much is 'me' and how much is outside of 'me'. Are the spirits that Violet describes parts of her or are they separate entities? I know of no neat answer for this. I think they are both separate spirits and part of her because she has, in effect, called this energy to her so that it then becomes part of her until such time as she gains the strength to push it out.

A shamanistic way to look at this is that all the energies of life are out there in the non-manifest world and we act as channels. By our choices we open ourselves to channel energies. We can open the channel for compassion or rage or love or happiness or depression. That energy then enters and becomes 'me'. Spirit possession, as worked with in many African shamanistic systems, is the deliberate conscious opening to a chosen energy for a certain time only. Mediumship is the conscious opening to a spirit guide. In the Western way of thought, the issue of what is me and what is not is seen as very important, but in many other parts of the world it is of lesser import, as 'me' is just a point through which passes all sorts of spirits/energies/essences. It is interesting to note that time and time again a new invention appears in one part of the world and almost simultaneously and independently is made by someone else far away.

Violet continues:

And then by chance I read Leo's article on Trance-dance in the magazine *London and South East Connection*. It was a revelation. I had no idea such a thing existed, that my kind of dancing had a name, or that people met up to do it for the purposes of healing.

My introduction to Trance-dance: August 2000

My first dance was a sheer celebration of the joy of being alive, of dancing to, and with, the drums. I danced for the love of rhythm, of beauty, of my body and its freedom, and for love itself as the energy that moves the universe: My power animals, guides, masters, were all celebrating my joy with me, and I felt abundant love for everyone.

My second dance was entirely different. This was the blindfold dance with a partner: When I came to dance I found the blindfold strangely comforting. It really focussed me into the dance and into my thoughts and feelings. I found myself retracing my life as the imprisoned, mute, emotionally and spiritually tied-up woman, trying to get free, my arms wrapped round my body like chains. At one point I had hold of my wrist so tightly I could not physically pull my hand off. I released a lot of anger and frustration during this dance, stamping, punching the air, dancing tight-fisted and aggressive, but it gradually moved into a dance of freedom as spirits came and cut my chains with bolt-cutters, showered me clean and handed me a new, pure golden heart ... I asked to be shown my future path, and saw a golden road with a rainbow at the end, but the part nearest to me was overshadowed. I tried to move around these shadows, but was literally prevented from moving very far and the drums were dying down. My journey mirrored my physical situation and vice versa. I was angry, seeing my dance as unfinished, but then Leo's face appeared and told me to 'follow the drums, follow your heartbeat'. And I realised that of course my journey is unfinished – the path and the rainbow remain and the journey continues.

The drumming for the trance-dance sessions was amazingly powerful, and now I understand what is meant by the talking drum. The drums hold you, lead you in and on, pick you up when you tire; they shout back at you, sing to you, comfort you . . .

And both dances made me so very aware of the safety of that space. I have never felt able to dance like that in a group before, to be wild, to be crazy, to fully express the movement of my body. After years of holding myself rigid with fear, of being unfit and overweight, I could at last allow myself to be totally liberated physically . . .

The healing of that ecstatic energy continued to carry me flying along over the next couple of weeks, I barely touched the ground, and my senses were incredibly heightened. Then I experienced another downturn, and a very strong pull to return for the Advanced Trance-dance a month later.

'Advanced' Trance-dance September 2000

This time it was a very different but even more powerful experience. Even the sweatlodge was different, I had none of the fear I experienced the first time, and a most beautiful journey in which I shape-shifted from condor on the roof of the world to a fish leaping down foaming rapids, to a stag in a forest, into a multitude of crows and back to the condor on its high mountain peak.

The morning after the sweat we were introduced to the Bear Trance Posture . . . Suddenly Bear appeared in front of me on his hind legs, roaring. He then came behind me, paws on my shoulders, and at that moment, for the first time, I really let my body take over. I was jerked about, small spasms at first, mostly around my navel (where there was intense heat) and lower back, then my neck, which was violently jerked backwards at one point, and I realised it was some sort of alignment, a preparation. I noticed I was breathing very deeply, pulling more energy in with each breath. Then I got the urge to move my hands from the original position and to hold them out like claws, semi-clenched. As I did this the most incredible energy shot through each hand from the back to the palms . . . I asked Spirit what I should do with it, and was directed to channel it back into my solar plexus, then my third eye and temples. When the rattles finally stopped and the session ended, the energy continued, even when I sat down . . . My hands still felt like iron claws and I wanted to smell everything, I had to sniff my skin, my clothes, I could smell the grass, the sunshine and the breeze outside. After several minutes my hands gradually returned to normal, feeling small and 'flat'. It was a weird sensation and I stayed in this strange space for several hours, very connected to my senses, particularly touch and smell.

Later that afternoon came the Trance-dance . . . I was spun into the dance and went off as usual, dancing to the beat of the drums, but found that I couldn't properly connect with the rhythm. Then I saw Leo's face again, over my golden path, and heard the words 'listen to the Spirit of the Dance, let it dance you.'

So I did what I had done with the Bear Posture, I allowed my body to do its own dance . . . It quickly went into spasms again but this time it was very different . . . I quickly realised that this was the perfect time, the perfect space, to be rid of those demons for good. I was fully protected by the group, the helpers, my minders. My power animals and guides were also around me, but were holding back from direct intervention. This dance I had to do alone.

I danced for the whole hour and a half. It was a battle, a life and death struggle which I was determined to win. It began to form a pattern. I would get myself into deep trance by swinging my left arm into the beat followed by wild head-shaking. I was also breathing deeply, drawing energy in to give me more strength. I was then attacked from inside, often so violently I was flung about the floor, my body racked by the spasms. It must have looked painful, but the pain was experienced on etheric levels, not the physical.

When I screamed it was not in fear but frustration, because I knew I had to get them out . . . Then, after a particularly nasty attack and violent throw to the floor, I reached the limit of my frustration and anger at these things that had haunted me for so long. Operating on pure instinct, I bent over and literally worked them out by a combination of breath control (pulling them upwards) and my fingers, pulling them up my body in the etheric. I could feel exactly where they were, and I had worked them up to my throat and was half-gagging when someone appeared and took something away. Still in trance I was not fully aware what had happened, but my dance calmed down at once . . . At some point a spirit appeared and gave me a large baby, which I rocked and cuddled and absorbed into me. And then the drums died down. I was still afraid they were in me but I was totally exhausted. I felt unclean and my sweat smelled foul. Once able to stand, I could not wait to wash and change my clothes, but I was also numb, in shock, for the rest of the day.

The magnitude of this experience was only brought home during the sharing circle the following morning, when I told the group about my three-headed demons and the total despair I had been in for months. One of the helpers* reported that she had indeed pulled a three-headed entity out of my mouth . . . I was overwhelmed, not just by the knowledge that it was out of my system for ever, but that she had seen it herself. [And she later confirmed that a drawing I made of the demons back in June corresponded closely to what she had seen.] This was very important to me, it was confirmation that these things do exist.

*Vanessa Morgan and Alison Lees were co-leading the workshop with me. Vanessa went to aid Violet and performed an extraction pulling this entity out. She told me what she had done and later in the sharing circle Violet described exactly what Vanessa has seen and removed. That was the first Vanessa knew of Violet's experience. Violet continues:

I had tried all ways to rid myself of these demons. Shamanic counselling, spiritual healing, mediums. I have no idea how long they've been there, feeding on my despair, my anger, fear and self-doubt ... But I do know that the actual physical nature of the trance dance was the only way I could get rid of them ...

Under the conditions presented by the Trance-dance I could totally, completely let go and let the spirit dance me into taking responsibility for my own healing. Twenty-five years ago I screamed my agonies out in a cold white room, unsafe, unprotected, unguided and subsequently violated. Now, following this simple but incredibly powerful and ancient ritual, I am at last coming into my own voice and my own power. My life cannot be the same. Now that really is a transformational experience.

Postscript

The dance had not finished with me yet. Having extracted negativity there is a gap left to be healed and filled. Though still shattered by what had happened I was also aware of an urgency to fill that gap. The following morning a warm-up tape was played. Gazing out at the beautiful trees in the grounds I became aware I was slipping into trance as I moved gently to the rhythm of the music. I knew it must be for a good reason, so allowed it to happen ... Within five minutes or so I was completely absorbed into a wonderfully warm, comforting space. Then the group was organised into a circle dance ... As the dance and chanting began I fell into a deeper trance, moved into the centre and almost immediately found myself wailing with an anguish that seemed to come not just from my personal history, but from a more ancient place, all our ancestral grief. I then became attuned to the beautiful healing energy of the circle around me ... I saw myself growing anew from the earth, I knelt on the floor and felt the soil between my fingers, caressed golden heads of corn, the silkiness of flowers. I ran my hands through flowing water, felt the sun warming and nurturing me as I grew and grew until I stood on tiptoe looking up at the enormity of sky and universe . . . I am back in charge of my life, and my gratitude to those who made this possible cannot fully be expressed.

That is one person's story of transformation through dance. As you will have read, part of her journey involved a major extraction of toxic energy, so let us now look at shamanic extraction.

Extraction medicine

One of the medicines of the shamans is the ability to extract energies, energetic invasions, entities – one can name them in different ways but essentially they are our own repressed selves or else negative energies sent to us. The most potent tend to be old stuck energies of lost parts of ourselves which are so hidden that we do not know they are removable because they feel so much like a part of our self.

There is a problem of definition between cultures. For example, what is a 'bad vibe' in one is a 'bad spirit' in another. A good example of this problem happened many years ago when I had a client on a year-long course whose right hand would automatically cover her face whenever she tried to express her emotions. It was a completely automatic reaction and she could not control it. It left her with some degree of social problems and considerable difficulty in expressing her true feelings. Thinking that I did not know enough to really help her I took her to see a South American shaman who was available at the time. To my horror and hers he told her, 'you have an evil spirit inside you' and he said it would take ten sessions for him to remove it, but unfortunately he was not going to be around for enough time for that to happen. I did not doubt his ability, but in the circumstances I was left to help someone whose fear had now escalated. I did my best to translate that what is an 'evil spirit' to his culture is a 'personality problem' to us – that was the best way of saying it for her benefit. She was participating in an ongoing course with me and so I was able to keep working with her. What I did was simply to ignore all manifestations of this problem and to model that quite pointedly for the other participants to follow, thus taking as much energy away from it as possible. By the end of the course, with all the things we had done together and been through together and the very much greater self-confidence she gained, the problem simply melted away.

Our culture has ways of describing reality which are based on the assumption that only the visible, audible and touchable universe exists – hence the terms paranormal and extrasensory perception for what to earth-based cultures are neither para nor extra. We also have a very human-centred way of seeing the world which leaves little space for other kingdoms, other vibrations of being, other energetic influences to be included in the explanations of how things are. Earth-based cultures tend to experience and accept as normal things that our culture calls 'magical', or if really inexplicable our culture calls it the 'work of God'. We are really talking about the two very different visions of reality as described by Newtonian physics and by Quantum physics. The West sees Newtonian reality and the shaman sees Quantum reality. Both are true and both describe aspects of reality and we do best by holding both simultaneously, as all we have to do to change realities is change our level of working consciousness.

Psychology and psychotherapy tend to explain everything as parts of self, while shamans would consider many energies as coming in from outside. Hence however odd it might seem from a Western point of view, the extraction of energy makes complete sense from a shamanic point of view. Earlier we talked about addictions. An addiction can be seen either as a personality flaw or as an invasive energy which has taken a person over. My personal experience tells me that both views are partially true and that what starts as a liking for something – for example a drug like tobacco which has a very specific effect when inhaled – can later become an invasion by the spirit of nicotine when the smoker loses a part of their will to the weed. Serious drugs like heroin steal energy from a person in return for a false sense of security and a painless existence. But like the desert mirage, it is totally false. You become dependent on the substance which steals your life-force until you die or take back control.

Extraction medicine is an ancient tool of the shaman and the example in the story above is typical of what happens. It is a way one person can help another by interacting with their energy field in a beneficial way. A necessary talent is the ability to 'see' energy so vividly demonstrated by Vanessa. Because she was able to 'see' the invasive energy form, she could take the necessary action to assist Violet in her moment of need by extracting it.

Some years ago I had an experience of nursing a friend who had been through a spontaneous dramatic awakening. One can call it *kundalini* awakening, or an enlightenment experience or energy awakening, there are many possible labels. Essentially what happened was that her energy centres (*chakras*) opened wide and she perceived the universe as sparkling energy vibrations. The shock to her system was considerable as she had had no previous experience like it. While she was in and out of this state, I did numerous energy extractions under her instruction. She was very up and down psychically–emotionally as she processed all sorts of things about her life and she needed almost constant support. Extraction medicine proved very helpful in enabling her to release and she was able to guide me – 'left a bit, down a bit' – and when I got the right place and pulled out the intrusion, the change in her was instantaneous and remarkable. It was an excellent teaching for me to experience directly just how effective extraction medicine is.

Rave dance – techno-shamanism

This is a modern attempt to create tribal healing dances.

Our ancestors danced to connect to the pulse of Mother Earth and the cosmos. They danced to celebrate life and to cement the bonds of community. They danced to move beyond the boundaries of normal waking consciousness. They danced to activate the release of 'endogenously created morphine' – endorphins – the natural release of which brings feelings of pleasure and delight in existence – a deep sense of connection to the pulse of the universe.

The steady monotonous beat of the drum stimulates parts of the brain not normally affected in the everyday. It overrides other sensory input, blocking the left-hemisphere calculator brain, activates the reptilian brain, the mammalian brain and brings the lesser used nonlinear, intuitive, right hemisphere more to the fore. It opens the doors to the magical quality of the universe as an integrated pulsating oneness instead of a series of separate discrete objects.

Our culture has largely lost this connection but our youth and those less brainwashed by the status quo still long for it. Rave culture is a spontaneous expression of this deep desire. Hundreds of people dancing to the loud, all-embracing beat, entranced into the lesser-known parts of themselves, becoming unconditional, transcendent, a collective cry for freedom from the repression and drudgery that 'normal' life is for so many today. Rave culture spread like a wave through Britain, Europe and the USA, bringing people together to experience a dynamic dancing, moving, throbbing united oneness. It is important to understand that rave is not about pairing up, sexuality, getting it off, it is about community and unity – those essential needs so dramatically missing in much of current life.

Unfortunately, as with most things that get big, rave also has its downside. Uncontrolled drug taking, mixing ecstatic drugs with alcohol (a depressant), people spacing 'out' rather than 'in', the acting out of repressed anger, and so on. In the old ways, a community dance would take place in the context of ceremony with the medicine wo/man leading. The spirits would be called and the people guided to dance in a way of honouring – honouring the earth, honouring that which gives life, honouring the sun and the spirit forces that make this life possible. The ceremonial context, understood by all participants, would act to keep the dance congruent with communal aims for the good of all. Unfortunately those understandings and communal goals are no longer part of culture and so the rave scene inevitably gets its share of people who act out their anger and frustrations on themselves and others.

Some years ago I was asked to open a rave night with a circle for prayers and chants. This created a good feeling for the rave but as people tended to drift in over a longish period, it was attended only by a small proportion of the eventual numbers. I was saddened later to see some people out of their heads and alcohol flowing freely. I am totally against the mixing of alcohol with ecstatic drugs and, to me, no one in their right mind would do something so crazy. Alcohol frees inhibitions to a point, but it is a depressive and a downer. It creates a sense of separation, not unity, it releases fighting demons which can be seen acting out their stuff outside pubs at closing time, it opens doors of self-aggrandisement and false ego. Ecstacy (though dangerous) brings feelings of gentleness and lovingness – inclusion not exclusion – and a softening of boundaries and of ego.

It is interesting that the approved intoxicant of our culture should be alcohol and that more or less all visionary drugs should be banned. It is certainly logical that it should be so in a culture that prefers its citizens to be controllable. Alcohol steals personal power in return for a false sense of ego inflation and omnipotence. With that comes feelings of separation and thus the desire for competition and proving of the little self in comparison to other little selves. It also steals potency – the sexual potency of big drinkers may be enormous in their minds but it is very little in their bodies. Whereas the visionary hallucinogens (hallucinogen derives from the word hallowed) bring us a sense of unity, to a sense of sharing and giving, a desire for community and co-operation.

Many shamanic cultures have used and still use hallucinogens as their way of teaching those on a path to become shamans and also for their people to come together in ceremony and travel together to spirit realms. These are wrongly thought of as drugs, 'teacher plants' is a much better term as they are plants that can teach us. Just as plants feed us, clothe us, provide material for shelter, wood for heating and just about all our other needs, so some plants can also provide expansion of consciousness for the education of our awareness. Many plant remedies have been discovered by shamans who have learned to communicate with the plants' spirits who tell them what they are good for.

Strictly used under the direction of a shaman, who is a master of the plant, and for going into inner space and not just 'spacing out', a plant medicine will assist with the gaining of awareness and knowledge. In the Amazon basin, *ayahuasca* is the medicine used, a formidable teacher and purge as I have personally experienced. In the coastal regions of western South America, the San Pedro cactus is used and in Mexico and south west USA, the most common medicine is *peyote*, another cactus plant. All of them have the power to shut down the rational calculator brain and open up the visionary circuits and to make telepathy, distant seeing, intuitive knowledge, connection with and guidance from the spiritual worlds, the magical connected quality of the universe, all potent and able to be experienced.

In many ways the explosion of rave culture is an attempt to retrieve what has been lost and to find a way back to regular experience of transcendental states. Like most things nowadays it is flawed but it is nevertheless a brave attempt. My vision of hope is a rave with live African and Native American-style drumming, no alcohol whatsoever; circles of prayer, chants, spirit calling; and wild abandoned, self-less, ego-less dancing leading to a divine feeling of connection to All-That-Is and to the transcendent nature of existence. In a word – bliss.

For more information on the rave movement, read *Moving Into Ecstacy* by Amoda.

CHAPTER 9

The Twenty Count

Powers of the Cosmos as they affect human life

THE FUNDAMENTAL TEACHING that holds the medicine wheels and on which they rest is called the Twenty Count or Children's Count. It is said to be the way Native American children were taught to count because every power can be added, subtracted, multiplied and divided.

The Twenty Count is the most profound of teaching wheels and is worthy of a book or more on its own. Here at least is a chapter on it, and I want to convey its essence, to bring you a deep sense of it. I have been taught it by Hyemeyohshts Storm, Harley Swiftdeer, Joan Halifax and others. It seems that it originates from the Maya, though I feel its real origin goes back much earlier into the mists of old times. Certainly it was Storm who brought it to the Western world and he recounts his apprenticeship to a Mayan shamaness in his autobiography *Lightningbolt*:

The medicine wheel circle is the Universe. It is change, life, death, birth, and learning. This Great Circle is the lodge of our bodies, our minds and our hearts. It is the cycle of all things that exist. The circle is our Way of Touching, and of experiencing Harmony with every other thing around us. And for those who seek Understanding, the Circle is their Mirror. (Hyemeyohsts Storm)

175

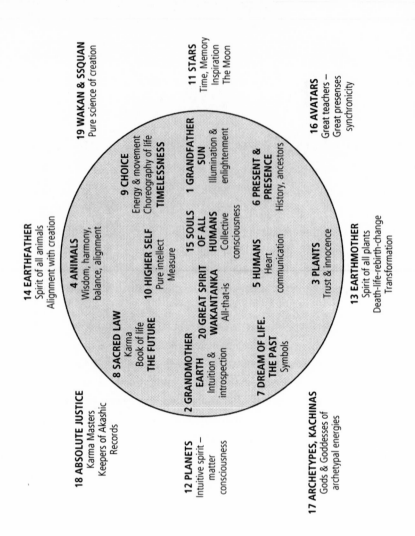

14 EARTHFATHER
Spirit of all animals
Alignment with creation

19 WAKAN & SSQUAN
Pure science of creation

11 STARS
Time, Memory
Inspiration
The Moon

16 AVATARS
Great teachers –
Great presenses
synchronicity

4 ANIMALS
Wisdom, harmony,
balance, alignment

9 CHOICE
Energy & movement
Choreography of life
TIMELESSNESS

**1 GRANDFATHER
SUN**
Illumination &
enlightenment

10 HIGHER SELF
Pure intellect
Measure

**15 SOULS
OF ALL
HUMANS**
Collective
consciousness

**6 PRESENT &
PRESENCE**
History, ancestors

8 SACRED LAW
Karma
Book of life
THE FUTURE

**20 GREAT SPIRIT
WAKANTANKA**
All-that-is

5 HUMANS
Heart
communication

3 PLANTS
Trust & innocence

**2 GRANDMOTHER
EARTH**
Intuition &
introspection

**7 DREAM OF LIFE.
THE PAST**
Symbols

13 EARTHMOTHER
Spirit of all plants
Death-life-rebirth-change
Transformation

18 ABSOLUTE JUSTICE
Karma Masters
Keepers of Akashic
Records

12 PLANETS
Intuitive spirit –
matter
consciousness

17 ARCHETYPES, KACHINAS
Gods & Goddesses of
archetypal energies

The Twenty Count

The Twenty Count is a circle of mirrors and a story of creation; it
starts like this:

In the beginning (is) was (and ever will be) Great Grandmother Wakan, the Great Round, the primal feminine, the potential of all things as yet unmanifest. The eternal no-thing-ness which is Everything, the Circle, the receptive-creative energy of potential, the yin, the zero. And simultaneously came Ssquan, Great Grandfather, the primal masculine, the yang, the lightning bolt, the sperm of creation, which enters the circle of Great Grandmother and potentises, the active-conceptive energy. The diagram below describes this moment.

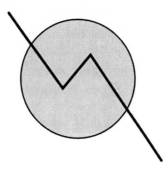

Great Grandmother Wakan and Great Grandfather Ssquan made love and gave birth to (for us in our neck of the universe) their first-born, Grandfather Sun, our Great Father.

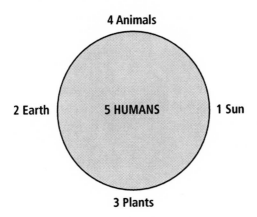

The cardinal 'holder' points of the wheel

1 Sun

His number is one and his place is in the east where he rises every day. His is the power of light, illumination, fire and warmth, the power that 'sees far' and lights up all things.

Great Grandmother and Great Grandfather made love a second time and their second-born is Grandmother Earth, our true mother and source of our physical being.

2 Earth (Gaia) Our Planet

Her place is opposite Grandfather Sun in the west and her sacred number is two. She holds the power of physical life, of introspection, of 'looks within'.

Now Grandmother and Grandfather made love and gave birth to their firstborn, the kingdom of the Plants.

3 The Plants

One plus two makes three and so their sacred number is three. Their place is in the south of the wheel where warmth comes from in summer. Theirs is the power of 'close-to' and of giving. The plants are stationary consciousness and they constantly seek to grow and to give of themselves without reservation. They have the power to change death into life.

Grandfather and Grandmother made love a second time and gave birth to the kingdom of the Animals.

4 The Animals

Their sacred number is four being the fire power of one added to the plants, three. Their place is in the north of the wheel. They have the gift of lungs, of heart and brain. Consciousness is no longer rooted in one place and so movement is birthed. This is the place of air, of the winds, of mind and thought. They are the ancestors of the humans.

Grandmother and Grandfather made love a third time and gave birth to their third-born, the humans, ourselves, the self-reflective beings of this world.

5 Humans

Our sacred number is five. We have the power of self-knowledge, of communication and language and our place on the wheel is in the centre, but south of the centre because we are as yet children and we are still learning to become fully conscious humans.

Hu means divine and *man* means means mortal. Humans are divine mortals in the sense that we have the gift of self-reflection, self-knowledge, the knowledge that 'I am'. The other kingdoms do not have that gift and so we are, in this specific sense, closer to the 'gods'. We are also yet to become fully human, the teachings tell us. We are on our journey learning to balance the forces of dark and light, to steer a course to become 'masters of energy', to know that we co-create our reality and that no-thing is actually here the way we perceive it – a terrifying thought. The teachings say that we are still children of the cosmos and thus our place is in the south until such time as we learn to work together, stop warring, and become caretakers of the Earth and each other, living with knowledge, balance, alignment, harmony and wisdom.

The first five powers from a human point of view

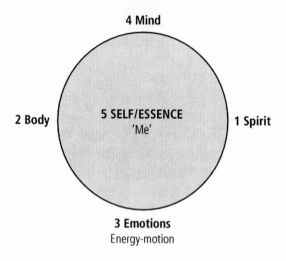

4 Mind

2 Body

5 SELF/ESSENCE
'Me'

1 Spirit

3 Emotions
Energy-motion

The human aspects of the first five powers

1 Spirit

Spirit, light, soul essence, visionary, seer, connection, intuition, illumination, genitals, semen, egg, creativity, action, masculine change. The light of the east is our essence, our timeless being, our 'seeing'. It comes forth as our creativity, our sex which creates our descendants, our ability to create change.

2 Body

Body, beautiful, Temple of The Spirit, movement, ugly, womb, testes, will, darkness, introspection, birthing. The dark of the west is our manifestation, our spirit incarnate in our walking body-temple, our soul.

3 Emotions

Emotions – energy-motion, waters, the seas, the rains, the rivers, all that flows, the blood in our veins; feelings, 'close-to', desires, movements towards change, towards fulfilment, fear, anxiety, shyness, inhibition versus trust and innocence, inner sense, inner essence, inner centredness. The watery emotional part of us that is rooted in the past through what we have learned. The energy-motion that impels us towards having our needs met.

4 Mind

Winds, storms, cool breezes, fresh air, stillness of the early evening, raging typhoon of the desert; 'knowing', thinking, awareness of future, beliefs, clear mindedness, lofty thoughts, low minded, courage, cour – rage, heart rage, anger to make things right and bring back lovingness. The mind which is intended to be our servant with its great calculating power but too often usurps the spirit and becomes our master.

5 Self/Essence

Balance, self, centre, knowledge of past and future, self-reflection, spirit, body, heart and mind in one being, the I is known, communication, doing, making. The centre where the 'will of God' (will to good) is known. The place of balance and harmony, humility and humour. Or the shadow which is an ego gone rampant.

The second five powers

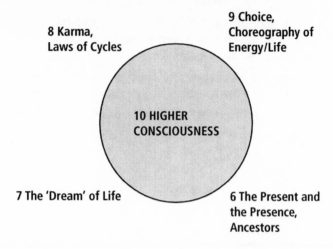

8 Karma,
Laws of Cycles

9 Choice,
Choreography of
Energy/Life

10 HIGHER
CONSCIOUSNESS

7 The 'Dream' of Life

6 The Present and
the Presence,
Ancestors

The non-cardinal 'mover' points of the wheel

6 The present and the presence, ancestors

To the power of five, the human being, add the light of one, Grandfather Sun. All that is born into substance is born from spirit. In the timelessness of spirit we are in the *now*, we are fully present. Hence when we are fully conscious and present while in body here on earth (not an easy achievement), we then can experience the presence of life, our presence in life.

This is also the place of the ancestors, all who have come before and who have made our lives possible, those in whose paths we follow. Through our ancestors we come to be. Our presence is only possible because of the past, and all who have gone before affect our presence mightily. Their greatness and their smallness lives on through us. Their blessings we inherit and their problems become ours to heal.

Hyemeyohsts Storm puts it this way. A human is a five, and when centred in the energy of five, the centre of the self, will consider all things from that place. Add one and that is how the human is present (six) in the world. So when centred in five with the added power of one (illumination), a human is fully present as a centred human. When centred in one, sexuality and the base centre, a human is run by their bodily desires and is slave to their sex rather than its master, and thus will be present (six) in the world in a very different way.

7 The 'dream' of life

To the power of five now add two, the Earth. When a human walks upon the Earth, s/he is living the 'dream'. We all know that earthlife seems very real and feels as if it is all 'out there', solid and happening. But from the point of view of the shamans, and quantum physicists too, 'no-thing' is really out there at all. Thought affects energy and thus what we experience. When the quantum physicist experiments, the attitude and beliefs of the experimenter tend to affect the outcome.

In the words of Carlos Castaneda's don Juan, 'we do not see reality, we only see a description of it'. That description is according to the myriad beliefs we have picked up since we left the womb. We are conditioned by a set of deeply held beliefs, and the universe kindly responds by proving us right. In the words of Henry Ford: 'Whether you believe you can or whether you believe you can't, you're right.'

All is vibration, waves or minute 'particles' that are not solid but energy in motion. All matter is energy, solid matter is *maya*, illusion, and yet earth life feels and seems so real. Einstein expressed this delightfully when he said, 'Reality is an illusion, albeit a persistent one.'

This is a very great paradox. 'Seeing' through the illusion is the ultimate aim of shamanic self-development work. The aim is to be able to 'see' the energetic reality behind the apparent reality, to see beyond the description of reality we have been taught and thus to be able to live in the really real world rather than the apparently real one.

The seven means much more than just night dreams. From Shakespeare (*As You Like It*, act 2, sc. 7), 'All the world's a stage [a dream], and all the men and women merely players [dreamers].' We create our world by our deepest beliefs of how it is. The shamans, the spiritual masters who do 'magic' have penetrated the veil, erased their personal (robotic) history, removed beliefs and worked to find knowledge and thus their world is not held as solid as for ordinary mortals. The learning of the seven is about becoming a creative dreamer of the kind of life you want to lead. The danger is of becoming lost in fantasy – just a load of old dreams that you never real-ise.

8 Karma, laws of cycles and circles, relationships

To the five now add three, the power of the plants, of emotion – energy motion, trust and innocence. A human, through experience of feeling the world, experiences karma, the law of cycles and circles, of action and reaction.

The eight is the one number which you can write repetitively over and over without taking pen from paper. Karma is action-brings-reaction, our lessons, the lessons we came here to learn, which the universe serves up to us over and over until we learn them. That is the universe's job: to educate us. Once we learn the lesson, we turn our karma into 'dharma' (to borrow a Buddhist term) – walking in balance, in 'The Way'. Now a new lesson will come to us, and so on and on and on.

9 Choice, choreography of energy

To the five now add the sacred four, the power of mind, of the wind, of the animal kingdom. A human being, through the reflective power of mind, experiences the power of conscious choice with awareness of effect (future).

This is the unique gift that humans have. The power of choice, of 'design and choreography of life-energy-movement – to use Swiftdeer's phraseology – the power to create and destroy. We are the 'determiners', and our life task is to learn to use that power wisely.

10 Higher consciousness, expanded awareness, higher self, spirit-knowing, pure intellect, measure of all intellect

To the five we now add five. Human plus human, the mirror reflection of ourselves. The ten is the 'measure of all intellect'. Intellect is the ability to measure in the widest sense of that. With this ability comes higher consciousness, expanded awareness, 'spirit-knowing'.

The second five powers from a human point of view

6 History, Ancestors, Presence

Negative aspects: Past – my personal history – my ancestry – past wounding – childhood trauma – soul loss – stuck energy – bitterness, anger, grief, disappointment, unfairness, regret, my emotional problems.

Positive aspects: It is also the present moment, the here and now, beyond past and future, beyond ego 'I'. In a state of egoless being, lost in the dance of life, I become the magical child, so engrossed in joyful existence that I don't know it because 'I' am not there to know anything. All is channelled through me and I am like a hollow bone. Six is all we have to let go of to be able to be just here, now and fully present in life. And it is that full presence, here and now.

7 The Place of Dreams

Negative aspects: My life-dream – the life I dream of versus the life I have dreamed into existence – reflections from life – am I the dreamed or the dreamer? – How awake am I to what I dream into manifestation? Who do I blame? Shame? Who's dream is it anyway? Not mine! Oh no

I never dreamed this. Couldn't be me, it's been done to me, them, my parents, God, the Devil did it. Definitely not me. Life's unfair, I never wanted it like this. I never did anything to make it like this.

Positive aspects: I am the dreamer. My life is my dream. I seek always to dream consciously so that what manifests is what I most desire in my deepest being for the best for all beings. I know my life is my dream so when it is not to my liking I look inside myself to see if there is some part of me that has dreamed it like this. I hold no blame because life brings constant challenges to my dream. I know the earth is sick and many beings are sick and wellness is something to be achieved and cherished. I hold to my dream no matter what comes to knock it away. I know that whatever comes to be, I will have dreamed my best with my full being.

8 Cycles and Circles

Negative aspects: It keeps coming round again – same situation, new people – new relationship, same problem – the pattern – my pattern – am I really the centre of my life – patterns inside – look across the wheel to six, my past, my history – my pattern comes from my history – my problems come from the past – blame, regret, shame, depression, dis-ease.

Positive aspects: Eight is life's teachings which challenges me to change my patterns, erase the shadows from my history, retrieve lost parts of my soul and bring dead parts of myself back to life. I awake to my karma, to what I have created by my actions, and I take charge of my karma to master my-self and learn the lessons life gives me. I accept life's lessons and change the patterns that no longer serve me. Let the dead in me be buried so the life in me may live.

9 Choice and Choreography of Energy

Negative aspects: It's all nonsense, I don't actually get to choose at all, 'they' stop me and limit me so it's not my fault if I can't make good choices, they messed me up and so I mess my life up but it's not my fault, they did it to me first. The government limits my choices, the tax man takes my money, there aren't jobs for people like me, what choice do I have? Don't talk to me about choice and free will, I just do it the way I was taught – my mother always did it this way – my father said that's the way you do it – I was educated to do it this way – I don't have a choice – freedom is a just bad joke.

Positive aspects: I am a conscious choreographer of my life and I take responsibility for my choices. I accept that life is learning and while I do my best to create a good life, I know that challenges and difficulties will come my way and it is my task to find the best outcomes. I tune into my higher self, my guides and helpers in spirit and I listen and learn. I take responsibility for my choices and how I design and choreograph my life.

10 Higher Consciousness

Intuitive knowing – higher self – higher intellect – the knowing of the spirit that we touch into when we connect to what is us yet more than us – the moments of synchronous just-knowing when that which we cannot know by ordinary channels is available to us. Electrified awareness – sparkling universe – in touch – more than the sum of my parts – guided – no egoism, no anxiety, just walking tall. Earth and sky, above, below and within me. I am, yet I am not just me and I am not alone.

A brief look at the next ten powers

All the numbers of this wheel add up, subtract, multiply and divide, and through this, they teach of relationships. Now we add the sacred power of ten, of higher consciousness, to all the powers.

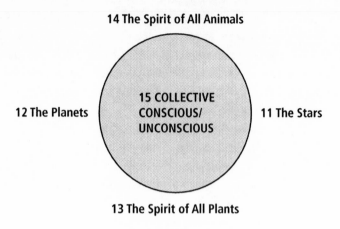

14 The Spirit of All Animals

12 The Planets | 15 COLLECTIVE CONSCIOUS/ UNCONSCIOUS | 11 The Stars

13 The Spirit of All Plants

The powers with higher consciousness

11 All the suns

One is our own Sun of God, so 11 is all the suns which is the stars. It is the spirit of all suns, of light and illumination.

12 All the planets

Add the power of ten to the two, the Earth, and we have all the earths. Just as two is our introspection/intuition, so 12 is the higher power of that, our intuitive spirit consciousness.

13 Spirit of all plants

Add the spirit (10) to all plants (3) – the green of the earth – making 13, the spirit of all plants. Every plant is a cell in the body of 13.

14 Spirit of all animals, sweet medicine

Add the spirit (10) to animals (4) and we have the spirit of all animals (14). Every animal, whether four legged, flyers, crawlers or swimmers, are cells in the great body of 14, known as sweet medicine.

15 Souls of all humans, collective consciousness

Add 10, higher consciousness, to the power of 5, the human being. The number 15 is the souls of all humans in and out of body, the totality of the human family. It is our collective conscious and unconscious minds, the total of the cosmic human thought-form. In this sense All-That-Is is part of 'Me'. It is the great 'I am' of human self-reflective consciousness.

18 Karma Masters,
Akashic Records

19 Primal Yin and Yang,
Pure Science of
the Universe

20 GREAT SPIRIT
CREATOR GOD

17 Weavers of The Dream,
Kachinas

16 Present and Presence,
Ancestors

16 Great presences, enlightened
ancestors, avatars

Add the power of ten to the six, the present and the presence, our history and our ancestors, and we have avatars. Those ancestors who became masters of energy, who found 'enlightenment' – the 'Great Joke of Life' – while alive in a human body.

17 Weavers of the dream that is life on earth,
archetypes, gods, goddesses

Add the ten, power of consciousness, to the seven of the dream and we have dream teachers, the non-manifest beings who teach us in the dream world, who guide us when we are in quiet, unbusy, relaxed, meditative states, who hear our prayers especially when they are truly heartfelt. These are the entities who guide the unfolding of the 'dream' that we experience as 'real life'.

18 Absolute justice, sacred law, karma masters,
keepers of the akashic records

Add the power of ten to the eight and we have the Karma Masters, keepers of Sacred Law, the Akashic Records (where all that happens is said to be recorded for eternity) and the Book of Life. These are the beings or energies who hold the laws of patterns and cycles at the highest level, the laws of how the universe works, how all the energy is held in patterns to create observable, experienceable 'reality', who keep karma, the balance of all things, and thus the ultimate absolute justice of the universe.

19 Pure science, design of all existence, goddess and god, primal feminine and masculine energies of the universe

Add ten to the nine and we add higher consciousness to the power of design of energy movement and choice. The 19 is the world of the Great Movers, the primal cosmic yin and yang or feminine and masculine. It is the pure science of the universe, the design of all existence, the 'mind of God'.

20 All-that-is, Great Mystery, Great Spirit, Creator God, infinity

Twenty equals $2 \times 0 = 00$ infinity, the Great Mystery, the Everything, made manifest in third-dimensional reality. It is completion, the double zero, and the potential of return to zero. The black hole of completion is also the big bang of initiation.

This is a brief exposition of this medicine wheel. There is a more detailed teaching in Hyemeyohsts Storm's wonderful book *Lightningbolt*. Storm brought these teachings to the Western world and as far as I know taught everyone who has subsequently spread the wonderful deep understanding and wisdom. There are depths upon depths in this teaching and I have only touched some of them here. My hope is that it will encourage you to seek further.

CHAPTER 10

Living shamanically

Beyond the consensus world view

To BEGIN TO BRING THIS BOOK to completion, let us take a moment to look again at our history and consensus cultural world view.

In the West we have a several centuries old agreement to view the world from a scientific materialist perspective in which events take place in the outer physical world in a literal and linear fashion. 'Newton's sleep', to quote William Blake. We have a working consensus that says the world is full of separate objects which interact in specified ways with specified results which can be scientifically demonstrated and proven. Speaking as a mechanical engineer (once an M.I.Mech.E – a full member of the veritable Institute of Mechanical Engineers), I can authenticate that this agreement works well for engineering. But engineering is not all of life and Quantum Physics shows a very different picture of the world. While in the everyday scale of things the engineering model works fine, at a subatomic level all is very different. Particles die and are reborn, they can be in two places at once, time can move backwards and effect can promote cause. The 'impossible', to the Newtonian view, is commonplace and happens all the time.

So let us knock a couple of consensus ideas on the head...

Paranormal

There is no such thing, it is all normal. By calling what the consensus sees as incomprehensibly 'para-normal', science manages to avoid facing the fact that there is a very great deal about 'normality' that is not understood. From a quantum physics point of view, the so called para-normal becomes pretty much explainable. The real world is nothing like the scientific-materialist description which is merely a convenience description for living within the parameters of the everyday. The real world is the one known and described by shamans for tens of thousands of years and is at last beginning to be described scientifically by quantum physicists.

Extrasensory perception

There is no such thing either! It is not extra, we all have perceptive abilities beyond the five ordinary senses, we are all psychic. The only question is how psychic we are naturally and how much we have developed these senses. Some are expert with well honed and practised psychic abilities, many are average and some are dunces – as in most things in life – but everyone is psychic to some degree, everyone is multi-sensed. Like every skill, it can be developed with practise. A much better title is EXTENDED SENSORY PERCEPTION.

THE DREAM THAT WENT WRONG

The Western technologically developed world was once a great dream of ease, prosperity, mastery over material things, ever more new work-saving inventions, shorter working hours, travelling and seeing the world, importing and exporting all the goods you could want from one country to another for plenty and variety, living with all you need at your finger tips, in luxury and ultimate happiness! Whatever went wrong?

Well, the great material prosperity turned out to be unsustainable by the planet. Our world is showing dire signs of strain and stress of the same kind that many individuals are suffering, and while some cultures are rich, many our still poverty stricken. Even in the 'developed' countries many are still living in relative poverty – we have collectively done nothing to even out the distribution of wealth. The happiness didn't materialise because the dream was conceived without care for limits of planetary resources and carried out with a mind-set of greed and competition rather than sharing and co-operation.

At the root of this is a great sense of disconnection from Mother Earth and the real source of spirituality, the Spirit-Which-Is-All-Existence. Both the creed of scientific materialism and the creed of dogmatic churchianity have contributed to the spiritual impoverishment of the people so now we have a society in which depression is a major illness. Apparently in USA, in the last 20 years while prosperity has risen 6 times, incidence of depression has risen four fold. According to the World Health Organisation, depression will soon be the second highest killer in the world. Depression is a product of a dream that may feed the body but doesn't feed the soul and it means that there is tremendous soul-loss taking place amongst the people. It means many people have lost their sense of connection, their sense of purpose of life, their reason for being. When the soul knows that the dream is unsustainable, that life cannot go on in this way, the young sense no future and take to ways of avoiding the deep pain which that causes. Hence the proliferation of drugs and alcohol, tranquillisers, sleeping pills and numerous ever more complex medications which temporarily hide the pain but at the price of life diminishing long term side effects.

Our challenge now is to re-dream and re-mythologise our lives and this means taking on full responsibility for ourselves, seeking real knowledge and letting go of the nonsense beliefs taken on from others, from popular orthodoxy, from what is actually nothing more nor less than mass mind-control. Twenty years ago I went to hear a man speak who in his turn had very publicly rejected religions and gurus and had stood alone, no matter what. Krishnamurti. He lived in Ojai, California at the time I was living in San Francisco. From my notes:-
"The followers destroy the leader and the leader destroys the followers. Buddha said don't worship anything so his followers worshipped him.

Humans create symbols and worship the symbols. Then the symbols take over. We need no mediators between Self and Truth. The difficulty is to 'read' the book of ourselves. To 'read' we need to take a careful look at our every thought and every action. We create gods and saviours out of fear. If we have no psychological fear we are beyond all 'gods'."

Also - I remember around twenty-five years ago being told the Hopi Prophecy at Third Mesa in the Hopilands in Arizona, by the stone where the motif is carved. It was a magical few hours. The Hopi Prophecy says (it takes four days to tell so this is putting just one aspect of it very simply) that as the ending times approach (of things as we know them), humans will divide into two streams – those who walk a 'one-hearted' path seeking unity with a deep sense of humility and those who walk a 'two-hearted' path with greed and selfish desire for domination. The prophecy says a time will come when the two streams will be so different that it will no longer be possible to move from one to the other. A very similar prophecy has come through the Findhorn Foundation in Scotland and there are numerous prophecies which say that Mother Earth is about to go through many changes including a change in vibration or a move to some greater evolved form. One thing is for sure - great change is coming and with it great challenge, that we can all sense. And it feels that the dividing of the ways is getting ever more stark between those who would live in harmony with the earth and the natural world and those who seek to dominate and control her and their fellow humans. We are all called to choose our path as this time unfolds and what we choose is of great import not just to our self but to the future of human life on planet earth.

HERE IS A CHOICE: SHAMANIC LIVING

The first responsibility of the shaman in ancient times was to keep the people 'in spirit', en-theos, enthused for life, with hope and direction and a sense of creative purpose.

So what does it mean for us today to live 'shamanically'? Firstly it means to live connected, connected to spirit, 'en-theos' – enthused, enlivened, vital, passionate; connected to Mother Earth and her other kingdoms; to the powers of the four directions and all those powers that make the reality in which we live. In so doing we move from 'alone and separate in a hostile Universe' to connected and part of a beneficent and loving existence. It is not that bad things don't happen – they are inevitable and act to balance the good - but that in seeing and feeling ourselves as part of All-That-Is, we are included and have a part in the play of it all. The bad things are lessons we are here to learn, the challenges that life gives us, the growth points, not the Universe's hostility but its inevitable shadow. From that point of view we can cope very differently with the demands that manifest. We take our 'right' back and live from an empowered place.

We knowingly walk both the Red Road and the Blue Road, and put our appropriate powers into each one. We live heartfully and purposefully on the Red Road, making loving connections wherever we can. Remember love can be hard as well as soft. Real love, care for the soul of another, can involve what seems mighty unloving at the time but will assist that person to awaken. On the Red Road, we embrace our full emotional and mental capacities, our talents and abilities to guide our-self on our Earth-Walk and create a good present and a good future for ourselves, our loved ones and All-Our-Relations.

On the Blue Road, we spend time in contemplation, in nature, in dreamy-time, allowing and listening. We have tools such as shamanic journeying to aid us to go within the matrix of parallel reality and give spirit the opportunity to show us knowledge and possibilities. We invoke our night dreams and ask them for guidance. We take ceremonial time-out to touch into the deeper reality beyond everyday concerns and to put ourselves in very different and perhaps challenging scenarios (a vision quest, for example) where we experience our-self in a unique situation from which we can learn much.

At a meta level it means constantly remembering that we are part of The Whole; that we do not exist as a separate being however isolated we may feel at times; that we are a cell in the body of Mother Earth who, in turn, is a part of the body of the Sun who, in turn, is a star in the Galaxy which is part of this Universe which is a part of.... And so it goes on. We have no separate existence, it is an illusion, we are minuscule pieces of the Great Mystery..

A GREAT MEDICINE WHEEL EXERCISE FOR LIVING SHAMANICALLY

To assist in re-mythologising yourself

Find a comfortable, quiet space, indoors or out, where you can be alone and uninterrupted. Create an eight-point medicine wheel with whatever is available to mark the directions, and make a space for yourself in the centre.

1. Face east and affirm yourself as Spirit-in-Matter, a part of All-That-Is, loved and cherished by Creation, on a journey of your own away from the centre where everything is known and out into the wilderness, the great unknown, where adventure and challenge is the order of the day.

2. Face south-west and affirm yourself as the dreamer of your life. You are the centre of your universe and you create, out of what is available on planet earth, your journey of experience.

3. Face the north. You hold your dream by the matrix of your beliefs, by how you hold the world to be in your mind. Consciously remind yourself that it is your dream and, while it will be impacted by others' dreams, you are the master and not the victim of how you experience reality.

4. Face southeast. By 'erasing your personal history' you accept yourself and who you have been so that you can now become who you choose.

5. Face west. By accepting death as your advisor, knowing that you are spirit and that only the body dies, you can dare to live fully and be fully present.

6. Face north-east and know it is up to you to choose your life-path. No one makes your choices but you. You are the designer and choreographer of your life.

7. Face south and affirm that you live in trust and innocence and without unnecessary fear, knowing the universe and yourself are one.

8. Face north-west and accept your karma, the life lessons you are here to experience and learn from. These are your teachers and they come in all disguises.

9. Face east one more time and remember you are spirit experiencing a life in a human 'vehicle of experience', as part of the Great Mystery which is All-That-Is.

The challenge to wake up

The human race is now challenged to wake up and to grow up. No more messiahs, no more 'gods' to die to absolve us of our responsibilities, no more 'belief systems' to come between us and our need to work out our own salvation and take responsibility for our actions. Here and now, at this time, we are challenged to return to the Garden of Instinctual knowledge and Oneness, and take with us the tremendous gift of our self-reflective consciousness.

We are all now called to what used to be the 'less travelled road', the road of personal inner development, of growing our awareness and consciousness, of taking responsibility for ourselves, our actions and our creations in the world, of working for our sister and brother humans, for the other kingdoms with whom we share the earth, and for our Mother Earth herself. Our evolution is our own task and our responsibility.

Bibliography

Amoda, *Moving into Ecstacy: An Urban Mystic's Guide to Movement, Music and Meditation,* Thorsons, 2001

Brown Jr, Tom, *Grandfather,* Berkley Books, 1993

Brown Jr, Tom, *The Quest,* Berkley Books, 1991

Brown Jr, Tom, *The Vision,* Berkley Books, 1988

Duffell, Nick, *The Making of Them,* Lone Arrow Press, 2000

Foster, Steven and Little, Meredith, *The Book of the Vision Quest,* Bear Tribe Publishing, 1980

Freke, Timothy and Gandy, Peter, *The Jesus Mysteries,* Thorsons, 1999

Harner, Michael, *The Way of the Shaman,* Bantam, 1980

Meadows, Kenneth, *Earth Medicine,* Element, 1989

Miller, Alice, *The Drama of being a Child,* Virago Press, 1987

Perkins, John, *The World is as You Dream It,* Destiny Books, 1994

Rutherford, Leo, *The Book of Games and Warm-ups for Group Leaders,* Gale Centre Publications, 1994

Rutherford, Leo, *The Way of Shamanism,* Thorsons, 2001 (previously published as *Principles of Shamanism,* Thorsons, 1996)

Sams, Jamie and Carson, David, *The Medicine Cards,* Bear & Co., 1988

Storm, Hyemeyohsts, *Lightningbolt,* Ballantine, 1994

Storm, Hyemeyohsts, *Seven Arrows,* Ballantine, 1972

Resources

For use with exercises in Chapter 6:

CD '*Drumming for the Shamanic Journey*' by Leo Rutherford and Howard G.Charing, published by Eagle's Wing Centre. Available from Eagle's Wing, BCM 7475, London WC1N 3XX. Tel: 01435-810233 or Bookspeed, 16 Salamander Yards, Edinburgh EH6 7DD. Tel: 0131-467-8100

CD '*Shamans of Peru*'. Field recordings of shamans of the Peruvian Andes and the Rainforest, their magical chants, icaros and indigenous music. Recorded by Peter Cloudsley. Available from Bookspeed or from Eagle's Wing.

CD '*Fiesta Music from Peru, 1980-2000*'. 61 tracks of unique music recorded as it happened, by Peter Cloudsley. Available from Eagle's Wing.

Eagle's Wing Centre for Contemporary Shamanism, BCM 7475, London WC1N 3XX. Tel: 01435-810233. Workshops, courses etc Website: www.shamanism.co.uk (Founded by the author)

Celebrating Woman, BCM 7475, London WC1N 3XX. Tel: 01435-810308. Website: www.celebratingwoman.co.uk Workshops and courses for women.

Sacred Hoop Magazine (UK shamanism / paganism magazine), BCM Sacred Hoop, London WC1N 3XX Website: www.sacredhoop.org Tel: 01239-682029

Sacred Trust PO BOX 183, Penzance, Cornwall, TR18 4QZ Website: www.sacredtrust.org Tel: 01736-331825

N'Goma Kundi (Shamanic) Drummers c/o 7 Martindale, East Sheen, SW14 7AL. Tel: 020-8876-9296

Spirit Horse Nomadic Circle, c/o 19 Holmwood Gardens, London N3 3NS. Tel: 020-8346-3660.

Deer Tribe Medicine Society UK. Website: www.singingstones.org Tel: 01433-651769

Vision Quest. The Way of the Inner Journey. David Wendl-Berry. Tel: 01453-828645. Email: david.wendlberry@ukonline.co.uk

Ehama Institute UK. Tel: 01736-333351. US: BOX 1205, Abiquiu, New Mexico, NM87510, USA. Email: ehamainstitute@att.net

Boarding School Survivors, Courses and Guidance,128, Northview Road, London N8 7LP.

Moving Centre UK, (work of Gabrielle Roth) Tel: 01803-762255 Website: www.5rhythmsuk.com

Jonathan Horwitz and Annette Host. Tel: 020-8811-2504 Website: www.shamancentre.co.uk.

Faculty of Shamanics. Website: www.shamanics.org. Tel: 01322-273364

Edinburgh Shamanic Centre, 288 Potrobello High Street, Edinburgh EH15 2AS. Website: www.shamaniccentre.com. Tel: 0131-657-5680

Hartwell Centre for Shamanic and Ceremonial Ways. Annie Spencer. Website: www.hartwell.eu.com. Tel: 01225-312728

Howard and Elsa Malpas. Shamanic Teachers. Tel: 07977-935633

Printed in the United Kingdom
by Lightning Source UK Ltd.
122667UK00001B/78/A